180
Prayers
For Your
Heart

Print ISBN 978-1-68322-378-8

Published by Barbour Books, an imprint of Barbour Publishing, Inc., 1810 Barbour Drive, Uhrichsville, Ohio 44683, www.barbourbooks.com

Our mission is to inspire the world with the life-changing message of the Bible.

ecpa Member of the
      Evangelical Christian
      Publishers Association

180 Prayers

OF A

Faithful Heart

BARBOUR BOOKS
An Imprint of Barbour Publishing, Inc.

Beautiful Are the
Prayers of a Faithful Heart

Quiet your heart as you reflect on these devotional prayers, each one inspired by Ephesians 1:15–23, and be drawn ever closer to the heavenly Father as you discover a deeper understanding and love for the One who holds the whole world in His hands.

Be blessed!

I have heard of your faith in the Lord Jesus and your love for all Christians. Since then, I always give thanks for you and pray for you. I pray that the great God and Father of our Lord Jesus Christ may give you the wisdom of His Spirit. Then you will be able to understand the secrets about Him as you know Him better. I pray that your hearts will be able to understand. I pray that you will know about the hope given by God's call. I pray that you will see how great the things are that He has promised to those who belong to Him. I pray that you will know how great His power is for those who have put their trust in Him. It is the same power that raised Christ from the dead. This same power put Christ at God's right side in heaven. This place was given to Christ. It is much greater than any king or leader can have. No one else can have this place of honor and power. No one in this world or in the world to come can have such honor and power. God has put all things under Christ's power and has made Him to be the head leader over all things of the church. The church is the body of Christ. It is filled by Him Who fills all things everywhere with Himself.

EPHESIANS 1:15–23 NLV

Strengthen My Faith

So do not throw away this confident trust in the Lord.
Remember the great reward it brings you! Patient endurance is
what you need now, so that you will continue to do God's will.
Then you will receive all that he has promised.

HEBREWS 10:35–36 NLT

Dear God, I need You. There are days when my faith slips away like a thief in the night, and I am unaware until I feel that emptiness inside me that signals life without You. Without faith my heart is hollow. Nothing can replace You there because I have given my whole heart to You. Renew my faith, Lord. Fill up my heart with Your unfailing love. When times hit hard and obstacles seem hopeless to conquer, give me hope. Remind me that trusting in You guarantees my reward in heaven. Reassure me that You are with me every minute of my day. Help me to endure the hollow times, and show me that they are a veil put there by the enemy to trick me into thinking that You have left me. I know, God, that You will never leave me. You have promised to be with me forever. Patient endurance is what I need now, patience in myself when I feel my faith wane and patience in You as You work out the plans that You have for me. Thank You, dear Lord, for hearing my prayer. Thank You for filling my heart with Your love.

In Jesus' name, I pray, amen.

What Is Faith?

*For this reason, ever since I heard about
your faith in the Lord Jesus. . .*
EPHESIANS 1:15 NIV

Dear Father, what is faith, really? What was it about the Ephesians'
faith that impressed Paul so much? What does that look like?

One dictionary defines faith as complete trust or confidence in someone or something. Your Word says faith is the substance of what we hope for, the evidence of things we can't see (Hebrews 11:1).

Ephesus was an important, prosperous city. People came from all over to trade silver and other expensive items. It also boasted many cultural opportunities. Like many big cities, Ephesus carried much corruption. The Ephesians weren't known for their quiet, wholesome lifestyles.

Yet a group of people there had embraced the Christian way of life. Despite their surroundings, despite their circumstances, despite the way they'd been raised, they trusted You. They had complete confidence that Christ was Your Son, and that He'd come to show them a better way. They knew no matter what happened, You were in control and You would take care of them.

Lord, I want to have faith like that. I trust You completely, even when I don't understand. I have confidence that You love me, that You're working things out for good, that You're kind and compassionate, and that You are in control. In the midst of a chaotic and corrupt world, I believe. I trust You. I have faith.

Faithfulness

But without faith it is impossible to please Him,
for he who comes to God must believe that He is,
and that He is a rewarder of those
who diligently seek Him.

HEBREWS 11:6 NKJV

Faithful One, thank You that You revealed to me that salvation only comes through faith in Jesus. I confess, even though I love Jesus with every fiber of my being, I am still so easily burdened by the cares of this world. I do not trust in You as I should. I plead for a bolder faith. You have proved Yourself time and again as the One who keeps His mighty and awesome promises. So I know You will keep Your promise that Your children will persevere. Even now, I know You are working in me a deeper faith in *Yeshua*—the God who saves. Let my faith be as great as a mustard seed, which, though it seems small, is all the faith Jesus requires. Let this faith move the dreadful mountains in my life that make me stumble or keep me from seeing Jesus. And when tests of faith come, as they surely will come, let me stand with the faith of Abraham in obedience, the faith of Joseph in suffering and purity, the faith of David to depend on Your strength and on Your forgiveness. Ultimately, may I be like Jesus in His faith to You, Father, while He was on earth: complete, unwavering, and fruitful.

Wisdom to the Weary Wolves

For this reason, ever since I heard about your faith in the Lord
Jesus and your love for all God's people, I have not stopped
giving thanks for you, remembering you in my prayers. I keep
asking that the God of our Lord Jesus Christ, the glorious Father,
may give you the Spirit of wisdom and revelation, so that you
may know him better. I pray that the eyes of your heart may be
enlightened in order that you may know the hope to which he
has called you, the riches of his glorious inheritance in his holy
people, and his incomparably great power for us who believe.

EPHESIANS 1:15–19 NIV

Heavenly Father, because of our faith in the Lord Jesus, we can't help but love our Christian friends. As we pray for one another, thankful for our companionship, remind us that we need the assembly of other believers. Keep us from becoming lax in our relationships. If we separate from the flock of Your sheep, we put ourselves and other believers in danger. The wolves of this world wait eagerly for one of Your lambs to step aside and falter. They find a way to justify their assaults on our beliefs when one of us slips.

But You, Lord, have offered us the wisdom in Your Spirit to thwart their attacks. You have shown us the path of light that leads far from their stinging barbs and toward the hope of Your higher calling. Let us extend Your light that they may follow us into an eternal inheritance, a loving relationship with You.

In Jesus' name, I pray, amen.

Called to Comfort

Praise God, the Father of our Lord Jesus Christ!
The Father is a merciful God, who always gives us comfort. He
comforts us when we are in trouble, so that we can share that
same comfort with others in trouble. We share in the terrible
sufferings of Christ, but also in the wonderful comfort he gives.
We suffer in the hope that you will be comforted
and saved. And because we are comforted, you will also
be comforted, as you patiently endure suffering like ours.
You never disappoint us. You suffered as much as we did,
and we know that you will be comforted as we were.

2 Corinthians 1:3–7 cev

Every person is hurting over something, Lord, so please help me to share Your comfort everywhere I see the need. A warm hug or sympathetic tears or simply a loving squeeze of the hand combined with genuine prayer for Your help have phenomenal power to heal and soothe. You've comforted and carried me through so many difficult times, Lord, and I am called to—and delighted to—pass it on. Help me, as I do pass it on, not to be overwhelmed in the midst of suffering. Your Word tells us we share in Your suffering, so we shouldn't be surprised by it. As hard as it is and as crazy as it sounds, help us to view suffering as a blessing because it always makes us more dependent on You, draws us closer to You. And thank You that You never allow us to suffer without sustaining us through it.

My Shepherd Friend

We are His people and the sheep of His pasture.
Psalm 100:3 nkjv

My personal, indwelling God, how can I live so far from You when You are as close as my breath? May I worship You and delight in You with my whole focus. Remind me to seek You as I read Your Word, because You desire relationship, not my Bible-reading ritual. Please give me opportunities to thoughtfully share Your Word with my family, coworkers, neighbors, and friends in a way that will bless them as You have blessed me.

You are my Good Shepherd. Help me to follow You closely, knowing that Your goodness and mercy surround me daily. Lord God, I find it hard to rest in fellowship with You. My mind scampers around You to jump on worries and wants instead. Then I gaze on cares of this world, and my heart stops grazing from Your green pastures. But You, the Father of glory, are my hope and glory. Cause me to know the richness of Your glory and my rich heritage because You have called me. Forgive me for avoiding You and straying away. Train my heart to long for You and my senses to thirst for Your still waters. Fill me with Your fullness, and be my all in all, so that I will not be at cross-purposes with You. I want what You want, even if it's not what I want! If it pleases You, it pleases me. Amen.

Loving Others

For God is the one who provides seed for the farmer
and then bread to eat. In the same way, he will provide and
increase your resources and then produce a great harvest of
generosity in you. Yes, you will be enriched in every way so
that you can always be generous. And when we take your
gifts to those who need them, they will thank God.

2 Corinthians 9:10–11 nlt

Lord, I confess that sometimes it is hard for me to let go of my own resources to help others. Yet Your Word tells me that You will not only provide for my needs but also supply for the needs of others through me.

This is such a paradox! "Give, and it will be given to you: good measure, pressed down, shaken together, and running over" (Luke 6:38 nkjv). If I truly love others, then not only my words but my actions also must show it. And the glory, and the thanks, all return to You.

Father, strengthen my faith to reach out to those in need. Help me let go of fears of being without, or not having enough for myself. Deepen my trust in You and Your promises. Help me walk in faith, believing You know my needs and will meet each one. Let my heart rejoice in thanksgiving for the opportunity to have a part in loving others and sharing the work You are doing in their lives. Amen.

Look to God for Answers

*Yours, O LORD, is the greatness, the power, the glory,
the victory, and the majesty. Everything in the heavens
and on earth is yours, O LORD, and this is your kingdom.
We adore you as the one who is over all things.*

1 CHRONICLES 29:11 NLT

Lord, You are from everlasting to everlasting. The cares of this world fall heavy on me at times. There is chaos, confusion, and so many people hurting in so many areas of life. Wealth and honor come from You. In Your hands are strength and power to promote and provide for my life and the life of every single person on earth.

I will not look to man or man's ways for answers. Truth and life come from You. You alone are my help and my comfort. I want to have a right attitude about money and giving. Give me a heart like Yours about money and provision.

All that I have today and all that I will ever have comes from You. Show me how to be a good steward with the things You have given me. In times of abundance, show me how I am to give generously. When things are tight, I know You are always faithful to help me make up the difference. As I am tempted to worry about the economy or finances, remind me that You are my Source and my Provider. You give me favor and blessing each day for the things I need.

The Love of God in Christ

I love you, Lord; you are my strength. The Lord is my rock,
my fortress, and my savior; my God is my rock, in whom
I find protection. He is my shield, the power that saves me,
and my place of safety. I called on the Lord, who is worthy
of praise, and he saved me from my enemies.

Psalm 18:1–3 nlt

Lord, Your eternal purposes have been accomplished through Christ. And now I can come to You with freedom and confidence. When I think of all this, I fall to my knees and pray to You, Father, the Creator of everything in heaven and on earth. I pray that from Your glorious, unlimited resources You will empower me with inner strength through Your Spirit, so that Christ will make His home in my heart as I trust in Him. My roots will grow down into Your love and keep me strong. Please give me the power to understand how wide, how long, how high, and how deep Your love is. Allow me to experience the love of Christ, though it is too great to understand fully. Then I will be made complete with all the fullness of life and power that comes from God.

Now all glory to God, who is able, through His mighty power at work within me, to accomplish infinitely more than I might ask or think. Glory to Him in the Church and in Christ Jesus through all generations forever and ever! Amen (adapted from Ephesians 3:12–21 nlt).

Wholehearted Commitment

*Let me say first that I thank my God through Jesus
Christ for all of you, because your faith in him
is being talked about all over the world.*

ROMANS 1:8 NLT

Lord, I wonder if people have heard about my "faith in the Lord Jesus" the way Paul heard about the believers in Ephesus in Ephesians 1:15. Do others know me as Your child? When they think of me, or hear of me, does my reputation tell them that I follow Your way, that I believe in Your Word?

Getting my feet and hands in tune with my mouth (what I do versus what I say) is probably the biggest challenge I have with this thing called faith. Believing means more than just knowledge or a philosophical nod of the head. It's putting your whole weight on a chair that you say is going to hold you.

Father, I don't want to be the kind of Christian who says "I believe" when my actions say "but not really." I want to wholeheartedly follow and obey You. I want to hold fast when others question. I want to completely trust You when others cannot see how You have proven Yourself over and over again. I want my life to shout to others that I am Yours, and You are mine.

Help me live each day reflecting You and showing by my actions that I believe and trust in You. Let the whole world hear about my faith! Amen.

Love for Those Who Hate

*"You have heard that it was said, 'Love your
neighbor and hate your enemy.' But I tell you, love your
enemies and pray for those who persecute you, that you
may be children of your Father in heaven. He causes his
sun to rise on the evil and the good, and sends rain
on the righteous and the unrighteous."*

MATTHEW 5:43–45 NIV

Dear Lord, how can I love those who hate You? How can I love those who persecute Christians and take away innocent lives? Yet, that is what You want me to do. When I see hatred and violence all around me, You remind me to love. What is love? It is You, Lord. You are perfect love. All of us are born from Your love and created by You. You made us to be equal. You, and You alone, God, hold the power to judge and condemn. You know what is hidden beneath the evil that fills human hearts. My task, the one that You have given me, is to pray away evil. So, God, give me the words to pray. Help me to look beyond the evil acts and pray for the hearts of those who need You most. When I think about the evil that humans do, remind me that all are welcome to the gift of Your salvation. Open their hearts, Lord. Fill them with light! Lead them to You. Bring them to their knees seeking Your forgiveness, and wash away their sins. Amen.

Love Like Yours

*Ever since I heard about your faith in the
Lord Jesus and your love for all God's people. . .*
EPHESIANS 1:15 NIV

Dear Father, that's kind of different. Paul heard about the Ephesians' love for each other? It's usually the fighting, the arguing, the backbiting. . .the *drama* that makes it through the gossip chain. I don't often hear about a group of people who really love one another. I wish I could be part of a church like that.

I suppose I can be, if I'm willing to love even when it's hard. After all, anybody can love others when things are easy. You said in 1 Corinthians 13 that love is patient. . . . Why would You have said that, if we weren't going to have reasons for patience? Why would You have told us to be kind, if kindness weren't a challenge at times? According to that passage, love is not easily angered, not prideful.

Love always protects, always endures, always hopes. Lord, do I know how to love? Does my life exhibit these qualities? I know I have a long way to go in some areas. Please help me to love like You love. Help me develop the qualities that will display the kind of love that comes only from You. I want to have a growing, blazing, contagious love that will spread to those around me and point them to You. Amen.

Love for the Saints

For we have a great joy and consolation in your love, because
the hearts of the saints have been refreshed by you, brother.
PHILEMON 1:7 NKJV

Lord of the Church, You have given Your people a new status.
Though we are sinners, You give us the title of saints when we
are justified by the blood of Christ. We praise You for the rich
heritage of the saints that went before us and the example that
they give us of steadfastness, courage, zeal, and above all, love.
Thank You for the saints in the Bible who, though in disagree-
ment over small things, remained united in Christ. Forgive me
for taking this title of saint for granted, and give me a renewed
zeal and love for Your people. If I forget or wander from Your
path, I pray that You send the love and care of present-day saints
to guide me back to You. As I read Your Word, let me not skim
over Paul's greetings to the saints of his day. Show me the beauty
of his fellowship with them and how important it is to care for
fellow believers. Reveal to me how I may serve and love the
saints today. Let my spiritual gifts be used for the edification of
the Church. And when our time on earth is done, may we come
resting from our kingdom labor, shining in bright array, to our
King. Then we will hear Him say: "Well done, good and faithful
servant. Enter."

Supplication for God's Saints

Wherefore I also, after I heard of your faith in the Lord Jesus, and love unto all the saints, cease not to give thanks for you, making mention of you in my prayers.

EPHESIANS 1:15–16 KJV

Heavenly Father, my heart grows heavy when I hear of our fellow Christians who suffer disparagement and injury, even death, in defense of their belief in our Savior. Many of them have given up personal safety and comfort to stand up for their faith in the Lord Jesus. You called these devoted saints into their distinctive ministries, and I give thanks every day for their relentless obedience. The example they have set for other believers gives me the courage to pass on Your good news to my neighbors, my coworkers, and other acquaintances.

Please let Your presence be known to our Christian missionaries in these troubled times as You strengthen them in faith and bolster their love for Christians around the world. I pray they will feel Your loving arms around them, and accept the inner peace only You can provide. May Your triad of graces—faith, hope, and love—bless them in their tireless efforts to proclaim their faith throughout the world.

Knowing You are with them in their efforts lifts the weight of sadness from my heart. Help me rejoice with them each day as they persevere for the sake of the Gospel of Jesus Christ. For it is in His precious name that I pray. Amen.

My Unbelief

So He asked his father, "How long has this been happening to him?" And he said, "From childhood. And often he has thrown him both into the fire and into the water to destroy him. But if You can do anything, have compassion on us and help us." Jesus said to him, "If you can believe, all things are possible to him who believes." Immediately the father of the child cried out and said with tears, "Lord, I believe; help my unbelief!"

MARK 9:21–24 NKJV

Heavenly Father, time and time again I have seen Your hand at work. Again and again You have proven Yourself trustworthy. I *do* believe in You. I believe in who You are and in all Your power. I believe that nothing is impossible for You! I believe You are good and just and holy and that You are working with a master plan.

Like so many things, though, faith is much easier said than done. It's easy to say I believe, especially when life is good. But it's so desperately hard to really act in faith when all seems lost or the obstacles seem impossible.

Oh God, in the darkness, when I'm overwhelmed and doubting You, please shed Your light on my circumstances. Remind me who You are. Keep my focus on Your promises. Soothe my anxiety with Your peace. Please, Father, strengthen my faith in You and *help my unbelief.*

Applying Wisdom

We have not stopped praying for you since the first day we heard about you. In fact, we always pray that God will show you everything he wants you to do and that you may have all the wisdom and understanding that his Spirit gives. Then you will live a life that honors the Lord, and you will always please him by doing good deeds. You will come to know God even better.

COLOSSIANS 1:9–10 CEV

Father God, oh how I need Your wisdom! I struggle with so many decisions in this life and often the way seems very unclear. When I'm uncertain, I feel like the "double-minded" man in James 1:8 (NIV), but You promise to reveal Your wisdom if I ask in faith.

As Paul prayed for believers all through the New Testament, so I pray, Lord, for wisdom and understanding of Your power and greatness. Wisdom goes beyond knowledge. Wisdom is knowledge gained by experience; it is good sense or judgment. Wisdom is experiential—it is meant to be acted upon. It goes beyond simply "knowing" something and gets to the heart of understanding it.

That's so true for my spiritual walk, Lord! I read Your Word and "know" all about You and Your ways. I may *know* many things—but what do I *do* with that knowledge? That's wisdom. Help me gain knowledge, apply wisdom, and obey Your Word so I can come to know You "even better." Amen.

Rule over Me

Exalt the LORD our God, and worship
at His footstool—He is holy.
PSALM 99:5 NKJV

Come, Lord Jesus. Come to this troubled and twisted world—right the wrongs, and give us peace. All rulers and principalities, power and dominion are under Your authority, but they rebel against You. They refuse to bow at Your feet even though all things are under Your feet. The earth is Your footstool, and You are head over everything. You are head of the Church universal—the body of redeemed saints worldwide and history long. May we all live to the praise of Your glory.

Forgive me when I do not want You to be my head. When I don't welcome Your authority or let You rule my life and desires. Lord, wean me from myself. Forgive my rebellious ways and independent spirit. Trying to run my own life doesn't work. I give up my plans and goals, the hopes and dreams I have for myself and my loved ones. Take my expectations and longings, my treasures and precious things, my burdens and anxieties. I submit my struggles to You. My victories and successes belong to You. Subdue my failures and fears. I rest in Your sovereignty and bow to Your will even when it hurts me. Thanking You for unwanted assignments does not mean I appreciate them—it means I accept them. I am restless on this earthly journey but confident in my destination. Even so come, Lord Jesus. Amen.

In Times of Doubt

But those who trust the Lord will find new strength.
They will be strong like eagles soaring upward on wings;
they will walk and run without getting tired.

ISAIAH 40:31 CEV

As You know, trusting others doesn't always come easy to me. I should be able to trust You, God, 100 percent, but there are difficult times that cause me to doubt. Forgive me when I struggle with that. There are people who have failed me, but You have never failed me—even when I couldn't see how things were going to turn out.

You never promised that everything would be easy. You even said in Your Word that there would be trouble, even as Your child. But You have promised that those challenges will not consume me as long as I lean and rely on You. Even in heartache or tragedy You can turn it to my good.

I choose today to trust You, no matter what the circumstances look like. You said there is nothing I can do—no circumstance in life—that will separate me from Your love. Help me to look to You and You alone. Take my hand and lead me through the difficulty. As long as I have walked with You, You have never left me without hope. You have always provided a way of escape. You always keep Your promises, and so again today, I place my trust in You!

For This Reason

For this reason. . .I have not stopped giving thanks.
EPHESIANS 1:15–16 NIV

Dear Father, I have so many reasons to give thanks. Like Paul, all I have to do is stop and think, and I come up with a near-endless list of things I'm grateful for.

It's so easy to focus on the things I'm not thankful for, Lord. People disappoint me. Circumstances overwhelm me. I lose my keys or sleep through my alarm, and life frustrates me. Day after day, hour after hour, negative things compete for the valuable real estate in my mind.

I'm not the only one with difficulties in my life, though. Just look at Paul. He had horrible memories of his past, of which he was deeply ashamed. He was imprisoned for doing what he felt called to do, what he felt passionate about. He was punished for living out his love for You, Lord.

Despite all that, he found reasons to give thanks. His writings are positive and uplifting, and his encouragement reaches far beyond the intended recipients of his letters. They reach beyond his time and place, through the centuries, to the other side of the world.

Father, I want to be like Paul. I want to smile and give thanks and focus on the good in my life. I want to be an encouragement to the people around me.

Thank You, Father, for so many good things in my life. Amen.

Deep Thanks

We give thanks to You, O God, we give thanks! For Your
wondrous works declare that Your name is near.

PSALM 75:1 NKJV

Sustainer of all, You created everything out of nothing. You brought light where there was darkness and healing where there was brokenness. You have come down Yourself. You suffered and died so that I could become whole again. I praise You that I am fearfully and wonderfully made in Your image. Thank You. Forgive me for taking thankfulness lightly. You have given me everything. You gave me Yourself, God Almighty, in the flesh. Thank You for the joyous times of beauty and love. Thank You also for the difficulties, which You use to mold me. I am so grateful for the Holy Spirit through which You do this sanctifying work. Thank You that You give me more than I can ever ask for or imagine. Thank You for the Church, for fellow believers—for our mutual encouragement and challenges. Thank You that You are not a genie who fulfills my every demand, but as a Father You know exactly what I need. Thank You for Your gentle and rough chastisements, which bring me back to where I need to be in my walk with You. Thank You for the assurance of salvation for all who believe. Your name is clearly emblazoned in the smallest comforts and Your presence powerfully felt, turning even mundane things into objects of beauty. Thank You that You are wondrous and Your wonder never fades.

The Gift of God's Light

"The sun will no more be your light by day, nor will the brightness of the moon shine on you, for the LORD will be your everlasting light, and your God will be your glory."

ISAIAH 60:19 NIV

Oh Lord, I miss out on so many of Your little blessings. When I become entwined in my daily tasks, I forget to look for You. But then You open my eyes, and You shine Your loving light upon me. Every day, I see Your light all around me. I awaken to a magnificent sunrise with colors that rival the best artists' palettes. Your sunlight brightens my day and it warms me. Your light shines in children's laughter and the kind acts of strangers and friends. I see it in smiles shared and comforting words and in friendship. All through the day it shines. And when the sun sets, Lord, Your light goes on. You set the moon in the sky to softly light the earth. You scatter the stars across Your black velvet canvas. You call each star by name. I look at the night sky, and I know that You exist beyond it. I imagine Your heaven, a place where the sun always shines. And when I turn off the light before I go to sleep, I am never in darkness, because You, God, are my everlasting light. When the sun, the moon, and the stars go out, when Earth's light fails, Your light will shine forever. Amen.

Show Me Your Ways

Show me your ways, LORD, teach me your paths.
Guide me in your truth and teach me, for you are
God my Savior, and my hope is in you all day long.

PSALM 25:4–5 NIV

Show me Your ways, Lord. Guide me and teach me the truth. Help me to put my hope in You no matter what. I think about Job and all he endured. He lost everything, and yet he still put his trust in You. He was stripped down to nothing and even his health was failing. His wife told him to curse You and die! Yet Job still held on to the hope that You were sovereign and that You were with him. You were faithful to Job and restored to him all that was lost and more. Job said, "I had only heard about You before, but now I have seen You with my own eyes" (Job 42:5 NLT). Help me to have the kind of faith that Job had.

I know my faith will be tested in many ways as I live life in this fallen world. Continue to guide me in Your truth. I know I will fail at some point, and I am so thankful that You are gracious and compassionate, slow to anger and rich in love. Your grace is sufficient for me. Your power is made perfect in weakness. I believe as the scriptures say "when I am weak, then I am strong" (2 Corinthians 12:10 KJV). I know that strength comes from You alone. Thank You, Jesus!

Wisdom, Please

If any of you lacks wisdom, let him ask of God, who gives to all liberally and without reproach, and it will be given to him.

JAMES 1:5 NKJV

Dear Father, a good friend is in a predicament. Please help her find a place to live soon. Her lease is up in a week, and she didn't renew. She believes she should downsize to cut her expenses. I know she's right, but so far she doesn't have a place to go. As a single mom, she feels the weight of responsibility.

It seems she's forced to take an apartment that's not exactly acceptable. She called me to pray for her as she goes to make application and pay the nonrefundable fee. I pray for wisdom and peace for her. This whole situation overflows with stress. She doesn't want to lose the fee, but she feels this must be Your will because there isn't anything else. Is that true, Lord?

Many voices scream when we try to change habits. "You're doing the wrong thing!" "You've got to do this now!" "You're going to fail!" I know. I've heard those same lies.

Lord, I ask that You speak to her heart. Calm her with the assurance that You'll take care of her and her son. She believes that, but I detected a bit of panic in her voice. She didn't ask for my opinion. She asked for Yours. Steady her. She desires to follow Your lead. Counsel her, Holy Spirit.

Called Unto the Fellowship

*Wherefore I also, after I heard of your faith in the Lord
Jesus, and love unto all the saints, cease not to give
thanks for you, making mention of you in my prayers.*
EPHESIANS 1:15–16 KJV

Gracious Lord, thank You for surrounding me with loving family members and friends who share my faith in You. We gather together on different days of the week to study Your Word and to pray for one another. You brought us together for such a time as this: to store Your Word in our hearts, to edify one another, to share grief in our losses, and to celebrate one another's joyful events. And to give thanks to You for this wonderful fellowship of believers. As we encourage one another, let our lights shine so brightly that bystanders will see how genuine our love is for You and one another.

Please help us to remain steadfast in our faith and love for Jesus. It's so easy to go astray when our work and personal business pull us in different directions. Give us frequent promptings during the day as we fold laundry, change diapers, teach students, or engage in business to remember that You are always with us. Remind us to look to You for guidance in our everyday tasks, including our leisure activities.

Thank You for granting me the privilege of coming before Your throne of grace to pray for these precious saints.

I pray this to You in the hallowed name of Jesus. Amen.

An Invaluable Inheritance

I often think of the heavens your hands have made, and of the moon and stars you put in place. Then I ask, "Why do you care about us humans? Why are you concerned for us weaklings?" You made us a little lower than you yourself, and you have crowned us with glory and honor.

PSALM 8:3–5 CEV

When I consider how often I neglect my relationship with You, Lord, I am ashamed. I live on this amazing planet and watch the stars beyond number in the sky, and fail to be awed by Your greatness and power. The fact that You love us, or would even have anything to do with us, is amazing! Yet more days than not I take that for granted.

Let me say now with the psalmist, "O LORD, our Lord, how excellent is Your name in all the earth" (Psalm 8:1 NKJV)! Let me marvel at Your greatness and power. May I be struck with the realization of what Your love for me means.

God, You have elevated man to a position of extreme importance—You offered Your only Son's life for ours. You bestow on us honor and glory and offer us an inheritance of indescribable value—eternity with You. You have shared all that You have—all that You are—with me who is so unworthy! Father, remind me of all that You have done for me that I might in turn reflect that love to others. Amen.

Vocation

And let us not grow weary while doing good,
for in due season we shall reap if we do not lose heart.
GALATIANS 6:9 NKJV

Sovereign Lord, You see how difficult it is to do Your work. I am
a fallen creature in a world that is in rebellion against You, its
Maker. When I go to do Your kingdom work, numerous obstacles
are thrown at me and I see Satan trying to discourage me. Help
me not to give in to my weaknesses. Do not let me get tired of
doing good for others, but give me renewed strength. Fill me
with joy as I serve others and especially as I serve the saints
and seek to love fellow believers. Let my heart remember and
feel that as I bless others I am also blessed. As I labor in Your
kingdom work, keep my eyes focused on the harvest. When the
time comes, let me be ready to bring in the sheaves. The fruit of
work done for You is the sweetest. Remind me that when I do
the work You called me to, I am only then truly being my whole
self. When opportunity arises for me to do Your work, do not
let me shirk the responsibility. Give me boldness to grab hold of
the task and do it to the best of my ability. Then I will feel Your
pleasure, which is the only thing that gives true joy. Keep me
and Your Church from growing weary.

Always Rejoicing

Rejoice evermore. Pray without ceasing. In every thing give thanks: for this is the will of God in Christ Jesus concerning you.
1 THESSALONIANS 5:16–18 KJV

Dear Lord, help me see the good in every situation, in every season of my life. Your Word tells me to rejoice always, but honestly some days I get so focused on stress or hurt or hardship that it's hard to find any reason to simply smile, let alone rejoice. The silver lining that's supposed to be in each cloud that comes my way isn't always very shiny.

In those times when I'm struggling to find any joy, help me to stop and gain a better perspective. I know I have plenty to be thankful for. I have so much to rejoice over and praise You for. I have life and breath and promises from You to provide for every need and to never leave or forsake me. Help me to realize that You are all I need. Every other good thing in my life is simply an added bonus because I have it all in You!

Keep me in constant communication with You. And thank You that You, the God of the universe, want to be in constant communication with me. When I keep my focus on that fact, when I keep my focus on You, how can I help but rejoice always? You are amazing, God!

Compassion for Others

According as he hath chosen us in him before
the foundation of the world, that we should be
holy and without blame before him in love.

EPHESIANS 1:4 KJV

Lord, sometimes I struggle to see the good in people. I can be quick to judge. Then I remember all I was before I knew the great sacrifice You made for me. I pray You will let me see them through Your eyes. All You have done for me, You have also done for them—even if they have not accepted Your gift yet.

I was dead in my sin, but You have made me alive in Christ. So when others do things that offend me, help me to forgive them because You willingly forgave me. So many times I disappointed You, but You responded in mercy. Help me to show mercy to those who disappoint me. There was a time when I followed the world instead of You. I pray that those who don't know You will find You, just as I did. Help me to stand for truth and believe that someday those who choose deceit can know Your truth as well.

I stand in faith now, praying that those deceived by Satan will find freedom in Christ. That they may know Your love and learn to serve You. Pour out Your compassion and love into my heart so that I may respond with a heart of wisdom toward those You give me opportunity to point toward You today.

Watch Jesus

We must keep our eyes on Jesus,
who leads us and makes our faith complete.
HEBREWS 12:2 CEV

Dear Father,

Our world—okay, my world—is distracting! Rush here. Rush there. Multitask. Street construction. TV. And then there's technology.

I'm always feeling behind. The rug needs vacuuming. The car needs washing. I ought to check email and Facebook at least three or four times a day. After all, I'm on two prayer teams. I must call friends. Set coffee dates. Where is that get-well card I bought yesterday?

I think I may talk too much when I get together with friends. I should try to listen more.

Oops! I seemed to have veered off track. Distracted again.

Urgency is a thief! Lord, I want to live life deliberately. Not haphazardly, worn out from attending to the next squeaky wheel. Help me prioritize. And, please help me ignore the snarky voice that whispers, "You're going to be late. You should have left five minutes ago. Hurry!"

Maybe if I would keep my eyes on Jesus, anxiety couldn't gain a foothold. Otherwise it's all about me, working hard to please who? Whom? (See? Distracted again.)

Jesus, because of You I don't have to allow distractions to pull me off course. Your Holy Spirit will lead me. I can trust Him. What's important today? I've got my to-do list, but what's Yours? A widow has been on my mind lately. It's time to call her, isn't it? I'll begin my list with her.

My Sacrifice

Offer your bodies as a living sacrifice, holy and pleasing to God—this is your true and proper worship.

Romans 12:1 niv

Gracious Father, You have chosen me to the praise of Your glory. You have sealed me with Your Holy Spirit, making Your promises sure. You have guaranteed me an inheritance with all the redeemed for the praise of Your glory, and yet You call us saints Your inheritance, even though You have done it all! These truths overwhelm my thoughts and emotions. How can I not offer You everything about me? I'm sorry for my fears that cause me to hoard the little I have. Fearing that if I give all to You, I will be deprived or lose out, that I'll regret it or won't have enough for myself. But sometimes it's my pride that dishonors You. I think that I am giving You so much, and You will be needy if I don't give it. Oh Lord, help me to live neither scared nor arrogant.

Give me true and proper worship. I act as if You offer drops from a fountain instead of the abundant river of life. I don't need to make You love me—You are lavish with Your love. You gave Your only Son for me. How dare I think You will withhold anything else that I need? God, You are merciful to me, a sinner. All I can do is give back that which You have first given to me. Amen.

A Plea for Wisdom

If any of you lacks wisdom, you should ask God, who gives
generously to all without finding fault, and it will be given
to you. But when you ask, you must believe and not doubt,
because the one who doubts is like a wave of the sea,
blown and tossed by the wind.

JAMES 1:5–6 NIV

Lord, make me wise. Open my heart, and allow me to know You.
Explain who You are beyond what You have revealed in Your
Word. Show me the depth of Your power. Show me the greatness
of Your love! Where my eyes have been blind, allow them to see.
Fill me up with Your knowledge. Ply me with questions and supply
me with answers. Teach me Your truths. Instill in my heart a
moral compass aligned with Your desires. Give me the wisdom
to know how and when to share You with others. Give me the
tools to unchain their hearts. Make me wise in faithfulness, Lord.
Teach me to trust and to believe in You without doubt. Make me
spiritually wise in battle. Harden my heart against evil, yet give
me wisdom about how to love my enemies. Advise me about how
to raise my children as children of God. Make me a God-wise
spouse, employee, leader, and friend. Lord, make me wise. Give
wisdom generously, forgiving me for my sins. I thank You, Father,
for Your goodness and love, and in Jesus' name, I pray, amen.

Continually in Prayer

Dear brothers and sisters, I urge you in the name of our Lord Jesus Christ to join in my struggle by praying to God for me. Do this because of your love for me, given to you by the Holy Spirit.

ROMANS 15:30 NLT

Lord, as Paul prayed over and over again for other believers, help me to enter into the "struggle" of other believers as well. Is not this the heart of love for them? How telling that scripture says this love is given by the Holy Spirit. That means I can't, Lord—but You can!

Paul says, "Keep on praying" (Romans 12:12), "My spirit is praying" (1 Corinthians 14:14), "You are helping us by praying" (2 Corinthians 1:11), "We have not stopped praying for you" (Colossians 1:9), "Never stop praying" (1 Thessalonians 5:17), "So we keep on praying for you" (2 Thessalonians 1:11), and "I am praying that you will put into action the generosity that comes from your faith as you understand and experience all the good things we have in Christ" (Philemon 1:6, all NLT).

Our prayers for others demonstrate our love, not only for them but for You, Lord. Help me to be consistent in lifting up the needs of others. The physical and material needs are important, but the spiritual needs are critical to living a life of faith. Continually praying for those needs is an expression of my love for others, and ultimately, an expression of my love for You. Amen.

A Prayer of Blessing and Protection

*Let love and faithfulness never leave you; bind them around
your neck, write them on the tablet of your heart. Then you
will win favor and a good name in the sight of God and man.*

PROVERBS 3:3–4 NIV

Fill me with love and faithfulness, Father. Write Your love on
my heart, and help me to love You with all my heart, soul, mind,
and strength. And help me to love those around me, even when I
don't feel like it. Give me bold, enduring love that is a testimony
to Your greatness.

I pray that I would find favor with You, Lord. And I ask that
You would bless me and my family. Just as You blessed Jabez
when he prayed: "Oh, that you would bless me and enlarge my
territory! Let your hand be with me, and keep me from harm so
that I will be free from pain" (1 Chronicles 4:10 NIV).

I pray that Your will would be done in my life, Lord. And that
I would be used to accomplish Your purposes in my life. I pray
that Your hand would be with me and that You will protect me
and my loved ones. I pray that You would keep us from the evil
one and give us strength to dodge our enemy's arrows.

The Precious Gift of Wisdom

*I have not stopped thanking God for you. I pray for you
constantly, asking God, the glorious Father of our Lord
Jesus Christ, to give you spiritual wisdom and insight
so that you might grow in your knowledge of God.*
EPHESIANS 1:16–17 NLT

Our glorious Father, we turn our ears to listen for Your wisdom
and open our minds that You may give us understanding. We
cry out for discernment and the ability to follow Your counsel,
and You answer our heartfelt plea. The spirit of wisdom reveals
Your perfect insights, which breathe new life into our weary
souls and help us to grow in our faith in the Lord Jesus Christ.

I fervently pray that all of us whom You have called will
be open and receptive to Your leading. We must be alert at all
times to shun the whispers of false teachers, keeping our focus
on You and Your Word.

I give thanks for Your vigilance as You direct us to follow
Your guiding principles, showing us how to live in a way that
pleases You. When we step off the narrow path, You rebuke
us—sometimes gently, sometimes firmly, but always in love—to
draw us back in line.

Help us to remember that only when we value Your gifts of
wisdom and insight as hidden treasures of gold or silver can we
find the true knowledge of You. Let our greatest joy be in worshipping You. I pray this in the wonderful name of Jesus. Amen.

Steadfast in Prayer

*Continue earnestly in prayer, being vigilant in it with
thanksgiving; meanwhile praying also for us, that God
would open to us a door for the word, to speak the
mystery of Christ, for which I am also in chains.*

COLOSSIANS 4:2–3 NKJV

Abba, let me never cease to come before You in prayer. You are
my Father and I need to be in constant communication with
You. Thank You for opening my eyes so that I see how I am
rejuvenated when I take time to talk to You. Let me regularly
come before You as a daughter and a friend. When I wake each
morning, remind me to first enter into communion with You.
And when night comes, let my weary day end in joy with You.
Keep me steadfast in prayer. Thank You that even when I do
not know what to say or how best to pray, the great Parakletos—
the Comforter who is the Holy Spirit—teaches me. Help me to
continually pray for my heart to be more like Christ. Just like
Paul, let me always pray for fellow workers in the vineyard, so
that whether far or near, we can carry one another's burdens
and fellowship through prayer. For the lost, help me to remain
vigilant and to petition constantly for their salvation. Thank
You, Father, that You know everything before I tell it to You,
but that this does not make my prayer any less important. Let
me pray without ceasing because I need to talk to You.

How Wide, How Long, How High, How Deep!

And may you have the power to understand, as all God's
people should, how wide, how long, how high, and how deep
his love is. May you experience the love of Christ, though it is
too great to understand fully. Then you will be made complete
with all the fullness of life and power that comes from God.

EPHESIANS 3:18–19 NLT

Father God, I often feel like I don't deserve Your love for me. It's unconditional and relentless. It pursues me when I pretend I can do without it. It accepts me and forgives me and welcomes me back repeatedly. Sometimes I feel sure You should just give up on me, but thankfully You never do. I can't imagine where I'd be if not for Your unfailing love, and it's impossible for me to put into words how grateful I am for that.

I know I will never understand Your love fully, but please help me keep experiencing it in new ways every single day. Surprise me with it. Sustain me with it. Comfort me with it. Satisfy me with it. Let it fill me up to overflowing—and let me share it with others! Help me to crave Your love above any other thing so that I am in constant communication and relationship with You through prayer and through Your Word. You are love itself, God. I praise You, and I love You back.

Sweet and Sour

For this reason, ever since I heard about your faith
in the Lord Jesus and your love for all God's people,
I have not stopped giving thanks for you.
EPHESIANS 1:15–16 NIV

Dear Father, I love the idea that Paul chose to give thanks continually for this group of faithful, loving people. I know people like that, but too often, they're not the ones who consume my thoughts and attention.

Instead, I'm prone to focus on the negative things, the negative people in my life. They're like gnats. . . I feel like I'm always swatting them away. I wonder what would happen if I chose to give them less space in my thoughts. If I pushed the negative things in my life to a corner and chose instead to focus my time and energy on the positive people, on my blessings, I'll bet my stress level would decrease.

Not that I should totally ignore negative people and things. Those people need my love and prayers. Those circumstances need my attention. But You want me to have sweet peace and joy and an abundant life. I can't know that sweetness if I'm constantly chewing on something sour.

Help me find the proper balance, Lord. I want to show Your love to negative people. But teach me to dwell on the positive people, the blessings You've placed in my path. Help me to never stop giving thanks for them. Amen.

Forever Faithful

*And the prayer of faith will save the sick, and the Lord will
raise him up. And if he has committed sins, he will be forgiven.
Confess your trespasses to one another, and pray for one
another, that you may be healed. The effective, fervent
prayer of a righteous man avails much.*

JAMES 5:15–16 NKJV

Heavenly Father, I never want to discount Your faithfulness
to me, Your child. There are times when I feel like You haven't
heard my prayer because I don't see changes. James 5:16 says
the prayer of a righteous person has great power as it is working.
I trust that You are working behind the scenes—doing things I
cannot see—to bring about Your good in my situation.

I repent for my own selfishness, focusing on what I want and
need. Many others need so much more than I do. As I pray and
hear from You, show me how I can pray for those around me.
Give me words to speak that will be a blessing to them. I open my
heart to hear from You concerning those around me. Share with
me how I can demonstrate Your love and faithfulness to them.

I trust that Your Word is true. That You are speaking to
my heart and giving me direction according to Your plan and
purpose for my life. But even more, help me to be a heart filled
with Your compassion for others. Even as I pray right now, I
grow in confidence knowing that my prayers make a difference.

Running to You

"He will rejoice over you with gladness,
He will quiet you with His love."
ZEPHANIAH 3:17 NKJV

My loving Father, I try to imagine You smiling and hugging me when I run to You. I need to disassociate You from my earthly father, who made many mistakes. I do forgive him, but old feelings cause me to question Your ways, doubt Your goodness, and try to avoid You at times. Please change these wrong concepts, so I will trust You with my heart, not only my mind.

Thank You for promising that when I ask for bread, You will not give me a stone. Even when it seems like You are not wise or loving (because I don't get my own way), I know that everything is for my growth, Your glory, and others' good. When You test me, it hurts, but it also helps. If Satan instigates evil against me, I do not fear him because You are head over all. You rule with authority and power. When You give me extra laps, You are a devoted coach, not a harsh taskmaster. You sometimes give me more than I can bear so that I will trust in You and not in myself, as 2 Corinthians 1:8–9 says. Help me to endure the race, fixing my eyes on You, avoiding distractions of the flesh and weights of the world, staying in bounds. May I finish well so I will be to the praise of Your glory. Amen.

Tenacious Love

*Nothing in all creation can separate us from
God's love for us in Christ Jesus our Lord!*
ROMANS 8:39 CEV

Dear Father, I can hardly stand to read, watch, or listen to the news. It's bad, screaming bad. Few news stories highlight uplifting situations. The immediacy of technology can make me feel like mayhem and destruction are always nearby. I could be the next victim.

Speaking of media, Christians are the one people of faith that it's okay to make fun of, lie about, or accuse of despicable things. How dare a professional football player, Hollywood star, or politician live and speak of his or her Christian beliefs. It's politically incorrect to utter the name of Jesus in a public place. Unless it's used as a curse word.

Another mass shooting meant to strike terror in the hearts of opponents. . .does. Are the domestic attacks committed by mentally ill individuals as we're told? Or are the ambushes strategically planned by determined enemies of freedom, of You? I'm reminded that we have an unseen enemy who is behind all acts of evil.

It feels like the world is coming apart at the seams. Wars, rumors of wars. Natural disasters. Vicious dictators. Murdered innocents.

Fear and despair stalk me to paralyze me. But, I won't succumb. No matter what happens, You still love me and are with me. Jesus defeated Satan at the cross. Instead of focusing on bad news, I'll look into the good news. Your truth will prevail!

A Prayer for Those in Authority

I urge, then, first of all, that petitions, prayers, intercession and
thanksgiving be made for all people—for kings and all those in
authority, that we may live peaceful and quiet lives in all godliness
and holiness. This is good, and pleases God our Savior, who wants
all people to be saved and to come to a knowledge of the truth.

1 TIMOTHY 2:1–4 NIV

Lord, I thank You for our Christian leaders—the pastors, ministers, priests, and others who understand that all things are under the authority of Christ. I pray for them always, and I ask that You supply them with spiritual wisdom and confident hope. When they face persecution and are tempted by evil, align them with You, Lord. Give them Your power to lead and endure.

I pray, too, for those who rule nations—chancellors, prime ministers, presidents, and kings. Turn their hearts right. Make them ambassadors for Christ, and give them the will to lead others in the ways of the Word.

Fill up the earth with God-fearing leaders: heads of cities and towns, providences, and states. Plant them in businesses, hospitals, service organizations, and schools. Make them the heads of households. Give them knowledge to mediate disputes, solve problems, love in all circumstances, and produce in others peace, quietness, godliness, and holiness.

And, Father, whenever You ask me to lead, whether it be at home, in the workplace, at church, or in my community, give me the wisdom to lead in a Christlike way. Amen.

Putting Aside Myself

Don't be selfish; don't try to impress others.
Be humble, thinking of others as better than yourselves.
PHILIPPIANS 2:3 NLT

I confess, Lord, that putting others first doesn't always come easy. It isn't hard to honor those who think of others before themselves, but what about those who are arrogant or in some way harder to love? That challenge is the one that gets me! And maybe, if I'm truly honest, I'm not so great at focusing on others' needs and wants and putting them first consistently.

Lord, I know You have called us to love beyond our own means to do so, but what does that mean in practical terms? I need Your help in living this out in my life—thinking of others before myself, putting their needs ahead of mine.

The first two verses of Philippians 2 tell us that Christ is the one who encourages and comforts us with His love. Isn't that what we are to pass on to others? The unity that Paul talks about in those verses is found when we love like Jesus did, and when we truly care about others, we are imitating Him.

I get it now, God—I have to think and act like Your Son. Please help me to think of others the way You do, to look beyond my own selfish ambitions. Lord, help me to show others love on a level that far exceeds my own. Amen.

Always Faithful

But the Lord sits enthroned forever; he has established his throne for justice, and he judges the world with righteousness; he judges the peoples with uprightness. The Lord is a stronghold for the oppressed, a stronghold in times of trouble. And those who know your name put their trust in you, for you, O Lord, have not forsaken those who seek you.

PSALM 9:7–10 ESV

Lord, You are always faithful. You never change in Your enduring love and justice. Nothing that has ever happened, is happening in the world right now, or will happen in the future is a surprise to You. You are faithful today, tomorrow, and forever. I can rest in the fact that You know all and that You are my stronghold.

When I'm in trouble, I can call on You. When I am glad, I can praise You. When I'm sad, You comfort me. When I'm happy, You rejoice with me. When I'm afraid, You wrap Your arms around me. And always I have faith that You are with me. You delight in me. You sing over me! I'm Your child and You are my loving Father in heaven. You are worthy of my constant praise no matter what the circumstance.

As Your Word says: Great is the Lord and most worthy of praise; Your greatness no one can fathom. I will meditate on Your wonderful works. They tell of Your power, and I will proclaim Your great deeds. I celebrate Your abundant goodness and joyfully sing of Your righteousness (Psalm 145:1–7 NIV).

Reveling in the Revelation of God

*That the God of our Lord Jesus Christ, the Father
of glory, may give to you the spirit of wisdom and
revelation in the knowledge of Him.*

EPHESIANS 1:17 NKJV

Gracious Lord, how often do I fail to seek Your wise counsel in my times of trouble. My search for answers on my own initiative always leads me off course. Like a boat without a rudder, I get tossed around in the ocean of doubt and uncertainty with my windblown attempts to resolve a difficult situation.

Sometimes I forget that the God of glory who appeared before Abraham and Moses is the same God who reveals Himself to me today—not verbally nor in the midst of a burning bush. Your Spirit speaks to me through the holy scriptures, which are filled with the glorious wisdom and revelation of almighty God. Please help me to not listen to my own self-centered pride, but to be more attentive to Your encouragement.

You reveal Your presence to me in things I see, hear, and touch, beckoning me to return from my wandering. How precious are the moments when I come back and surrender my empty efforts to You! As I leave my troubles at the foot of the cross, You enfold me with Your love and give me peace.

Thank You, Lord, for Your mercy and forgiveness, which are never ending. I lift this prayer to You in the name of my precious Savior, Jesus. Amen.

Strength for the Moment

Christ gives me the strength to face anything.
PHILIPPIANS 4:13 CEV

Dear Lord, it's happened again: another friend on hospice. It's so hard. I don't know what to say, and I'll pull into her driveway in about five minutes. The pain of possibly losing her breaks my heart. Of course, I know I'll see her again in heaven, but the thought of her leaving this life—my life—is so sad.

I'm bewildered, Father. I keep suppressing a bothersome question. It takes so much energy to hold it back. Anyway, it's not hidden from You. So I may as well acknowledge it. Here goes: Why? I don't understand why she's sick unto death. I don't. Nevertheless, from past experience I know You may not explain.

Okay. What am I sure of? You love her. Jesus will greet her when she's absent from her body. She will reunite with family and friends in heaven. And, she'll be pain-free. I can't help but smile. One day I'll make that joyful journey, too. Precious thought. My tears have subsided.

Thank You for the blissful sidetrack, but now I'm near her house. Only her sweet hospice volunteer's car is there, but she'll leave the room after I arrive. Help me put one foot in front of the other. Help me to string words together, and help me to listen. My dear friend's expecting me. I'm deeply grateful that I don't have to do this alone. And neither does she.

Wow Me with Your Power, God

*Now all glory to God, who is able, through his mighty power
at work within us, to accomplish infinitely more than we might
ask or think. Glory to him in the church and in Christ Jesus
through all generations forever and ever! Amen.*

EPHESIANS 3:20–21 NLT

Almighty God, please remind me of Your power. I tend to put You in a box, expecting You to work in only the ways I can think up. I worry through a problem, trying to apply only the figures and formulas that make sense to me, but that's kind of ridiculous—for You are the Creator of the universe, capable of so much more than I can possibly wrap my mind around. Your Word promises me You are able to do *infinitely* more than all I can ask or imagine.

Please wow me as You work in my current situation, as only You can do. Exceed all my expectations. Amaze me in a new way. Show me that absolutely nothing is impossible for You. I want to see Your hand at work, and I want to give all praise and honor to You. I want others to see Your miraculous ways, to witness Your almighty power, and I want You to receive all the glory!

Heart Needs

Give me an undivided heart,
that I may fear your name.
PSALM 86:11 NIV

God of my hope, it amazes me that I belong to You for all eternity, but life here is hard. Thank You for temporal pleasures, pleasant emotions, significant accomplishments, and meaningful relationships. But everything ages and atrophies. My heart must be set on pilgrimage, not on corruptible things. What I trust in place of You—people, possessions, activities, accomplishments, investments—is a counterfeit and an illusion. My joy is in You, not in what I do or who I love. I can rejoice in You, even when not feeling joyful.

God of my expectations, tame my wandering heart. I know that may necessitate a broken heart, but Your will be done. How easily distracted I am by self-seeking goals and my desire for approval from peers. I can realize the certain hope of my calling and the constant reality of Your power only when I fix my eyes on You. On Your glory, not my needs; on Your loyal love, regardless of my feelings. Help me to live devotionally, meditating on all You are and what You speak to me when I read Your Word. Although I fear trials and future sorrows, help me remember I can endure anything because You are always with me, Your Word is adequate, and Your grace is sufficient. Tears teach lessons I could not learn any other way. My whole heart loves You. Amen.

For Others to Know You More

*"Ask me for the nations, and every
nation on earth will belong to you."*
PSALM 2:8 CEV

Lord, today I pray for friends and family. I ask that You give each one the spirit of wisdom and revelation, so that they may know You better. Please open the eyes of their heart so that they can experience the hope to which You have called them. May they come to know the riches of their inheritance. I pray they realize all the rich blessing and favor You stand ready to impart to them as they each make You the Lord and Savior of their life.

For those I know and love who have questioned and maybe even walked away from their faith, I trust that You will find a way to bring them back into relationship with You. Speak to them in the nighttime. Bring up past memories of the times that You were there for them. Remind them of Your Word.

I think about each one of them as their faces come before me in prayer. You know where they are in their walk and what they have need of. Give me words to speak when I am with them that will encourage them in their faith and assure them of Your great love. May Your peace and comfort surround them, keep them, and protect them as they find their way back to You. I pray their journey starts even today!

Love

*For you, brethren, have been called to liberty; only do not
use liberty as an opportunity for the flesh, but through love
serve one another. For all the law is fulfilled in one word,
even in this: "You shall love your neighbor as yourself."*
GALATIANS 5:13–14 NKJV

Great lover of my soul, thank You for Your love that gives me
freedom, a love that casts out fear and removes doubt. Human
love is rarely constant, but I praise You for Your promise of loving
Your children with an everlasting love. Your love is able to take
away the debris of a rebellious heart and reconcile it with God.
You have asked us to emulate this perfect love, the love of Christ.
I am so weak, so full of pride and self-righteousness. Help me
to put others before myself. Must I live sacrificially? Yes, You
have shown me this, because it is the way Christ lived and it is
the truest of loves. When I see my neighbor in need let me be
bold and willing to serve. Just as important, open my eyes and
mind to love them not as I think they should be loved but to see
the best way of truly helping them. Thank You for Your perfect
love. Let my love for You grow, because only when I find You
as my first love can I learn to love those around me as I should.
Lord, You have loved the seemingly unlovable. I have no excuse.

Which List Am I On?

For this reason, ever since I heard about your faith in the Lord
Jesus and your love for all God's people, I have not stopped
giving thanks for you, remembering you in my prayers.
EPHESIANS 1:15–16 NIV

Dear Father, I'm grateful for many of the people in my life. I have been blessed with family and friends who love me, who make my life more pleasant in so many ways. Thank You for them, Father.

But there are also those people I'm not really crazy about. You know who I'm talking about, Lord. The ones who gossip and slander. The ones who complain all the time. The ones who look for the negative instead of the positive. It's hard to give thanks for them.

Father, I don't want to make lists for You of who I love and who I don't really like. You already know. I do, however, want to ask You. . .and ask myself. . .when others think of me, which list am I on?

I want to be the kind of person others are thankful for. I want to love so well, live so kindly, and laugh so freely that the people around me are glad I'm in their lives. Help me to live such a beautiful, faith-filled life that I'll be counted among people's blessings, not their curses.

I want to love like You, Lord. Amen.

Confident Hope

Guide me in your truth and teach me, for you are
God my Savior, and my hope is in you all day long.
PSALM 25:5 NIV

God, what would I do without You? When my spirit is weak,
You give me strength. When I feel hopeless, You flood my heart
with Your light, and You fill me up with hope. My hope is in You,
God, always and forever.

When I travel a road long and hard, You are there at my
side. You encourage me and keep me moving forward with hope.
When I face a task overwhelmed and worried, thinking that it is
too much for me, You give me hope and confidence to succeed.
And when night falls, silent and dark, You light my way with the
confident hope that morning will surely come.

Who would I be, God, without You? Hope in myself is not
enough. I fail, and my spirit falls desperate. But, You, God—You
give me hope! Even when the world says there is none, there is
always hope in Christ Jesus, Your Son. What a wonderful gift He
is, Your gift of hope to the world. He took all of my sins, died with
them, and then rose from the dead to give me hope. My hope is
in You, God, my trust is in Jesus. Thank You for the confident
hope that one day I will enter the gates of heaven and live there
with You forever. Amen.

Growing in Love and Knowledge

But I am like a green olive tree in the house of God. I trust in the steadfast love of God forever and ever. I will thank you forever, because you have done it. I will wait for your name, for it is good, in the presence of the godly.

PSALM 52:8–9 ESV

Heavenly Father, I *will* thank You forever! Anything good I have in my life is from You and for You. And the amazing thing is that You have even taken the bad and turned it into good! You turned my ashes into beauty and my shame into joy. You have promised freedom from chains. . .and peace from despair. You have faithfully fulfilled those promises in my life.

Like the olive tree, You are showing me how to grow in a healthy and right relationship with You and with others. You want me to flourish. You are for me, so who can be against me? It doesn't matter what anyone else thinks as long as I know in my heart that I'm pleasing You.

Help me to be strong in You when You ask me to do things that friends and family don't understand. Sometimes the cost of following You seems too much to bear. Please remind me that the rewards of following You are eternal. Keep me growing in the love and knowledge of You.

The Journey of Faith

Stop being hateful! Quit trying to fool people, and start being
sincere. Don't be jealous or say cruel things about others.
Be like newborn babies who are thirsty for the pure spiritual
milk that will help you grow and be saved. You have
already found out how good the Lord really is.

1 PETER 2:1–3 CEV

Lord, I've been on this faith journey for a while now, and the older I get, the more I realize how much I have yet to learn. Maturity brings the realization of just how much more growth I need. Sometimes I feel like I might even be regressing, needing to relearn what I've already been taught!

I don't want to be stuck as a spiritual baby, but rather to thirst for the milk of Your Word as Peter talks about—to grow in wisdom and knowledge—to have a discerning heart so that I hold fast to all that Your Word teaches. Lord, help me gain understanding of Your character, of who You are, and to stay focused on not only learning about You but on being transformed and changed by what I discover.

I am so thankful You are willing to help me! I know that growth can sometimes be uncomfortable and change can be painful, but I want to remember that these things are necessary and ultimately for my good. God, give me strength in heart and mind to continue on this journey of learning to know You. Amen.

Spreading the Spirit of Wisdom, One Person at a Time

That the God of our Lord Jesus Christ, the Father
of glory, may give to you the spirit of wisdom
and revelation in the knowledge of Him.

EPHESIANS 1:17 NKJV

My glorious heavenly Father, You are all-knowing and all-powerful, yet You offer each of us, individually, Your tender love. You created each one of us for a purpose: to know and love You as You know and love us. You have provided the perfect way for us to come to You through Jesus Christ. Jesus said that His Father is our Father, His God is our God, that we may understand the relationship You want us to share with You.

Thank You for giving the spirit of wisdom to my friend who presented Your Gospel to me when I walked in ignorance. My stubbornness melted away in the warmth of the revelation of Your love.

As I tell other individuals about this wonderful opportunity to know our Creator, please give me the sound judgment I need to not clutter Your message of love and forgiveness with my own ineffective words. Remind me I don't have to entertain them, or give the Gospel a colorful spin. You've given me all the words I need in the scriptures. Help me to steer people away from the lies this fallen world has to offer and direct them to the path of truth and wisdom that leads only to You.

I pray this in the name of Jesus Christ. Amen.

Enlightenment

*The eyes of your understanding being enlightened; that you
may know what is the hope of His calling, what are the
riches of the glory of His inheritance in the saints.*

EPHESIANS 1:18 NKJV

Great Reconciler, thank You for opening our eyes to the amazing
plan of redemption that has been laid out from the beginning.
When Adam and Eve sinned, their eyes were opened to the
terrible existence of a life separated from You. They saw death.
Let me, in Christ, see life. I do not want to live dead in my sins,
in blind rebellion against my Maker. Holy Spirit, remind me
that Christ has conquered death, and keep my eyes focused on
the beauty of the Gospel. Let no veil obscure my vision. May I
hold fast to the hope of being with God in eternity. Though now
I see as through a mirror dimly, then I shall see with the eyes of
Christ. Keep me faithful until that precious day when the last
of the sinful scales will fall, when my sanctification is complete,
and I can truly and finally understand: I was made to be with
You. If I am in danger of falling into darkness, shine Your light
of conviction and bring me to repent. You showed me that I was
blind; You have reconciled me to Yourself.

A Request for Humility

*Always be humble and gentle. Be patient with each other,
making allowance for each other's faults because of your love.
Make every effort to keep yourselves united in the Spirit,
binding yourselves together with peace. For there is one body
and one Spirit, just as you have been called to one glorious
hope for the future. There is one Lord, one faith, one baptism.*

EPHESIANS 4:2–5 NLT

Father, I confess that while I expect others to make allowances for my mistakes and faults, I am not always as patient with them as I expect them to be with me. Why is this so hard? Sometimes I think that I am getting it right, and then I find myself right back where I started—thinking of myself first.

To be "humble" is to not think of myself as better than someone else—it is deference, or submission, insignificance, and unpretentiousness. True humility is a discipline, Lord, and one I need help with. It is a way of life, a pattern of living in a way to consistently remind myself to allow for others' mistakes. It is learning that when I offer gentleness and humility to others, everything else falls into place exactly as it should be.

I know that unity with other believers will please You, Lord; it will bring peace with other believers and show those who don't know You a glimpse of Your love. Holy Spirit, enable me to live this out in my daily life. Amen.

Thanks for Encouragers

Therefore encourage one another and build each other up,
just as in fact you are doing. Now we ask you, brothers and
sisters, to acknowledge those who work hard among you, who
care for you in the Lord and who admonish you. Hold them in
the highest regard in love because of their work. Live in peace
with each other. And we urge you, brothers and sisters, warn
those who are idle and disruptive, encourage the disheartened,
help the weak, be patient with everyone. Make sure that nobody
pays back wrong for wrong, but always strive to do what is
good for each other and for everyone else.

1 Thessalonians 5:11–15 niv

Thank You, God, for fellow Christ followers who inspire me and help me in my walk with You. Please constantly place people in my life who will encourage me and build me up. Thank You for my spiritual leaders, for the pastors, elders, and teachers in my church, and for the friends and loved ones who guide and point me closer to You, too. Help them as they are leading others not to stumble but to constantly seek Your will in furthering Your kingdom. Help me to learn from them, to be teachable and open to their instruction. And help me to be as much of an encouragement to them as they are to me.

As I learn and grow, help me to be a good leader for others, as well. I want to live my life in such a way that You are pleased and so that others who know me want to love and follow You, too.

Eyes on the Blessings

All praise to God, the Father of our Lord Jesus Christ,
who has blessed us with every spiritual blessing in the
heavenly realms because we are united with Christ.

EPHESIANS 1:3 NLT

Thank You, God! I praise You and give You much thanks for the blessings You have given to me. I know I sometimes take things for granted, vent my frustration, and let disappointment overwhelm me. I want to see life through the blessings You have given me.

I could spend too much time telling You all the things I wish were better, different, or less than what I had hoped. I can sit in the dark and pout, but I know it is not Your way. I should come out into the light and give thanks. Each day I determine my attitude about my life and how I will respond. The choice is mine. I want to celebrate all the things that have brought joy and peace into my life.

Today I count my blessings. I have breath and life today. I have people who love me—and that includes You as well. I look back over my life and realize that You were always there, even the times I didn't feel Your presence. You have taken me on a journey, and You have made serious adjustments as a result of my own personal choices. No matter where I go or what I do—You are always there to show me the right path and bring Your blessings into my life.

Just Pray

*I have not stopped giving thanks for you,
remembering you in my prayers.*
EPHESIANS 1:16 NIV

Dear Father, thank You for Paul's example of praying for others. It's easy to pray about my own issues; I do that all the time. But I don't want to become so self-absorbed I forget to include others in my prayers.

The words are easy to say, Lord. "I'll pray for you." How often have I made that promise and then forgotten about it before I walked away? Forgive me, Lord. Hold me accountable to pray for the people You've placed in my heart. Hold me accountable to pray for the people I care about, and the people I don't really care for. Remind me to pray for my boss, my leaders, and my government.

In 1 Thessalonians 5:17, Paul tells us to pray without stopping. In James 5:16, James tells us that the prayers of the righteous are powerful and effective. At Your throne, we have access to Your power. Father, I want to take advantage of the opportunity You've given me to make a difference in the world. I can help implement positive change, simply by asking You. By talking to You. By telling You what's on my heart.

Thank You for giving me a voice with You, Father. Thank You for hearing my prayers and responding to them. Thank You for listening.

I love You, Father. Amen.

Strength and Joy

*We also pray that you will be strengthened with all his glorious
power so you will have all the endurance and patience you need.
May you be filled with joy, always thanking the Father.*

COLOSSIANS 1:11–12 NLT

Father, a dear elderly friend is experiencing terrible physical
pain. Some days are very difficult. This seems to be the worst
it's been in a long time. She asked me not to visit twice because
she wasn't up to it. She's never done that before.

This Christian woman is a wonderful example to me of
someone who, like Paul, has learned to be content whatever
the circumstance. She's housebound, widowed, and childless.
Yet, she hardly ever complains. One afternoon I told her that I
admired that in her. She said, "My mother always told us kids,
'Don't complain. No one wants to hear it.'"

When I visit her, I am blessed. Now I feel helpless in the
face of her pain. However, I'm not. Prayer is a strong defense,
not a last resort. Please ease her pain and strengthen her today
with Your glorious power. I pray that she is filled with joy. She
speaks often of You. Once she said, "I just don't know what I've
done that He's so good to me." An amazing comment. It's a
challenge to me.

I'm thankful that You brought us together. Other Christian
friends check on her by phone or drive her places. You've given
me the best job: weekly relaxed chats.

Sharing the Light

When Jesus spoke again to the people, he said,
"I am the light of the world. Whoever follows me will
never walk in darkness, but will have the light of life."
JOHN 8:12 NIV

Dear Lord, You are like a beacon of light that leads ships at sea. You light the way for the lost in the world. You give life to all who ask. Oh, how wonderful You are! You care about Your children, and You save them from death. Whenever they stray, like a good shepherd, You find them. You are their light in the darkness. "Come, follow me," You say, and then safely You lead them toward home.

I praise You, Lord Jesus. I praise You because You are the Light of the world and the light of my life. You keep my lamp burning. Every day, You flood my heart with Your love light, more than it can hold. I am eager to share it, so allow me, please, to help You to light up the world.

You are the only One who turns darkness into light. How can I share the light? How can I help the lost? What can I do to show them Your love? Lead me to them. Guide me to say and do what is right. Make me an example of Your light, and give me wisdom. Speak to me through Your Word, and help me to lead others out of their darkness so that they might live in Your light forever. Amen.

We Are Not Forgotten

Trust in the LORD with all your heart and lean not on your own understanding; in all your ways submit to him, and he will make your paths straight.

PROVERBS 3:5–6 NIV

In a nation that has fallen away from You—where violence is prevalent and the economy is unstable—I understand a little bit more of the prayer that Habakkuk cried out when he felt like You had forgotten his people: "How long, LORD, must I call for help, but you do not listen? Or cry out to you, 'Violence!' but you do not save? Why do you make me look at injustice? Why do you tolerate wrongdoing? Destruction and violence are before me; there is strife, and conflict abounds. Therefore the law is paralyzed, and justice never prevails" (Habakkuk 1:2–4 NIV).

I confess that I feel similar thoughts. I want to believe You haven't forgotten us, Lord. Please give me hope from Your Word. You were faithful to Habakkuk's people, and You kept Your promise to him. Give me that same faith today, Lord. Your Word tells me that You are the same yesterday, today, and forever. I have seen You actively moving and changing the hearts and actions of people throughout my lifetime, and I trust that You are still in control of all that is happening in our nation.

I pray for the leaders of our nation, that they would turn their hearts toward You and not lean on their own understanding. Help us as a country to acknowledge You in all of our ways so that You will make our paths straight.

Holiness

"Little Israel, do not fear, for I myself will help you,"
declares the LORD, your Redeemer, the Holy One of Israel.
ISAIAH 41:14 NIV

Holy Father, Holy Son, Holy Spirit. Holy, holy, holy. You are wholly set apart from sin in every way. And You desire me to be holy. You even name me a saint—a set-apart believer—only possible because You provided the substitute sacrifice that forgave my sins. You declared me righteous in Christ because I believed in Him for eternal life. Now Christ lives in me—may I not disgrace Him.

Redeemer God, help me separate myself from sin and be set apart to You. In fellowship, service, loving others, and in worship. Lord, multiply my love for You. Involve my whole heart, soul, mind, and strength. Increase my desire to love Your children and serve them. Wean me from judging them, from seeking their admiration, and from self-protectiveness that keeps me from reaching out to others. Without You, my love is nothing. Without Your enablement, my serving is nothing. And without Your empowerment, my holiness fails because I choose sin and self. Father, in the age to come I will be with You in glory—complete and sinless and perfect. Until then, help me to resist sin, say no to temptation, and deny my flesh. Enable me to evaluate choices biblically and to not let peer pressure conform me to the world. Help me live up to my name and be holy. Amen.

Shining God's Light of Love

My prayer is that light will flood your hearts and that you will understand the hope that was given to you when God chose you. Then you will discover the glorious blessings that will be yours together with all of God's people.

EPHESIANS 1:18 CEV

My Father in heaven, please help me to turn away from the dark shadows of this world. They are mysterious and enticing, but You are the glorious light whose radiance casts out the darkness.

I cherish the promise of hope, which You have given to all of us whom You have chosen. I stand ready in the charge of Your calling to let Your light shine through me. You have set me apart as a member of Your heavenly family. To be called Your child is so great an honor.

As my heart is flooded with the light of Your love, let me grasp the power of Your glory. Let me eagerly pore over and study Your good Word. And let my mind and heart be open to receiving Your inheritance, an immeasurable gift of legacy. Give me the strength I'll need to pass these timeless treasures on with joy to the generations coming behind me. They so desperately need Your light.

Thank You Lord, for showering me with the light of understanding, that I shall be able to uphold my faith in You. In Jesus' blessed name, amen.

Just Like You

I keep asking that the God of our Lord Jesus Christ,
the glorious Father, may give you the Spirit of wisdom.
EPHESIANS 1:17 NIV

Dear Father, they say a wise man learns from others' mistakes, a smart man learns from his own mistakes, and a fool never learns. I just have to shake my head at my own foolish mistakes, Lord. They're too numerous to count.

I do try to be smart. I try to learn from my own mistakes, and not repeat the same failures over and over. But if I follow You, if I study Your Word and listen closely to Your voice, I won't have to muddle my way through nearly as many fiascos. You will show me the way of wisdom.

Lord, I want to be wise. I know I'm not capable of perfect wisdom. . .I'm flawed, and You're not. But I do want to be just like You. When I cling to You, when I look to You for guidance and direction in each and every situation, I'll ride the coattails of Your wisdom and avoid futile mistakes. Even when I learn from my own mistakes, Lord, there's often long-term collateral damage. I'd rather not make those mistakes at all.

Help me today and every day to keep my eyes on You, and not get distracted by the foolishness around me. I want to be wise. Just like You. Amen.

Soothe My Troubled Heart

"Let not your heart be troubled; you believe in God, believe also in Me. In My Father's house are many mansions; if it were not so, I would have told you. I go to prepare a place for you. And if I go and prepare a place for you, I will come again and receive you to Myself; that where I am, there you may be also. And where I go you know, and the way you know."

JOHN 14:1–4 NKJV

Dear God, every time I watch, read, or listen to the news, I am deeply discouraged. Sin is making a nasty mess of this world. Some days I wonder how much longer this can go on! Honestly, I even wonder at times if You've forgotten us, forgotten Your promise to come back and get us and take us to the place You've prepared for us in heaven. Please fill me with hope when I'm feeling down and doubting You. Remind me of Your promises, and soothe my troubled heart. Help me to be patient and trust in Your timeline, confident that You are working out Your perfect will.

As I wait on You, please show me Your purpose for my life. I'm so thankful that my hope is in heaven and not in this broken world! Help me point others to salvation in You so that they will also share that wonderful hope.

Sister in Jesus

Love each other deeply with all your heart.
1 PETER 1:22 NLT

Dear Father, I hoped to see my Christian friend at the coffee shop this morning. I couldn't wait any longer. She's also a walker, so I decided to head toward her usual direction. Maybe our paths will cross in the shopping strip's parking lot. It's happened before.

I don't see any sign of her. The clock tower tells me that it's probably too late. That's sad. I may just go on home. Wait! There she is. She's got coffee. How did she do that? She must have gone in the back door as I went out the front. She's waving.

. . .Well, she was in a hurry, but she told me about their trip to Colorado for a pastors' conference. Her life is crazy busy. I've been praying that she could take some downtime so You can restore her soul.

She asked me to pray for refreshment. They're flying out today. I pray for a smooth departure from home and the airport.

Thank You for our brief conversation. Our meeting was no coincidence. You gave us those sweet moments together. I love her. Our coffee shop friendship is special because of You.

As You remind me of her during the next four days, show me how to pray for her and her husband. It's a delight and an honor to hold up dear friends to You in prayer. What a blessing to communicate with almighty God!

Help Me to Believe

*Therefore I will look to the LORD; I will wait for the God
of my salvation; my God will hear me. Do not rejoice
over me, my enemy; when I fall, I will arise; when I sit
in darkness, the LORD will be a light to me.*

MICAH 7:7–8 NKJV

God, there are times when I just don't see it and I really struggle
to believe it; but I know that You are the Great I Am. You will
not let me down. You will not fail me. So when it comes to those
really hard places in my life, I will trust in You. I will believe the
seemingly unbelievable. When others say "no way," I will say
"God has a way."

You have given me the ability to love because You promised
that Your love has been placed upon my heart. When I want to
respond in anger because of emotional pain, instead I can respond with love, by faith. There are times I fail and my feelings
get the best of me. During those times, I am thankful for Your
loving forgiveness.

Each time I refuse to stop believing, no matter how bad
things look, my faith grows. It's like a developing muscle. The
more the quarterback throws the ball over and over again, the
more his muscles are strengthened and he can throw harder
and farther each time.

Thank You for helping my faith to grow to a new level. Increase my faith, and help my unbelief as I grow to the next level.

Revelation

"I thank You, Father, Lord of heaven and earth, that You
have hidden these things from the wise and prudent
and have revealed them to babes. Even so, Father,
for so it seemed good in Your sight."
MATTHEW 11:25–26 NKJV

Eternal God, thank You for speaking to me through Your Word. I don't seek Your voice any other way, for that is arrogance. Your Holy Spirit can only illuminate the truths from Your Word that I read and have in my heart. Thank You for the instruction You give me from others You have gifted to share Your Word through sermons, songs, and writings. I seek nothing extra. Your Word is sufficient, and everything I hear or think or choose must be evaluated scripturally. Give me opportunities to show Your love and truth to others so they will be encouraged and edified. I need more boldness in this, so I pray for everyone I will encounter today—may I minister grace to each one through my words and deeds and attitudes.

Thank You also for showing me Your works in creation, in answers to prayer, in "coincidences," and even in interruptions. Lord, I trust You. Sometimes because I'm out of options, but mostly because You can be trusted. I trust You with my life and health, my wealth and well-being, my passions and goals, and my loved ones. Help me to depend on You for wisdom and understanding to know You intimately and love You intentionally. Amen.

Inheritance

Therefore you are no longer a slave but a son,
and if a son, then an heir of God through Christ.
GALATIANS 4:7 NKJV

Abba, thank You for making me Your child. You have bought me with the highest price and I praise You for giving me Your name. Why have You done this, Lord? Why give everything to people who constantly mess up? Thank You for Your Word, which answers, "Because I love you." When I tend to revert to my old life as a slave to sin and a son of death, beat at the door of my heart. Show me again the hope of a rich and glorious inheritance. How amazing to be an heir to the promises You gave Abraham and all Your children after that! Let me live as a child and heir should: full of love, hope, and peace. Thank You that as Your child You gave me Your grace so that I can live filled with these things. Make me sensitive to Your Spirit so that I do not shame Your name. You give Your children a higher name and status than the angels! I know nothing in myself is worthy of carrying Your name, which is above all names. But Your grace through Jesus has cleaned up the rebellious child in the pigsty. Thank You for the robe, ring, shoes, and fattened calf. Whether the road is short or long, keep me looking forward to my inheritance of eternal life with You.

Praising the Power of God

In that day you will say: "Give praise to the LORD, proclaim his name; make known among the nations what he has done, and proclaim that his name is exalted. Sing to the LORD, for he has done glorious things; let this be known to all the world. Shout aloud and sing for joy, people of Zion, for great is the Holy One of Israel among you."

ISAIAH 12:4–6 NIV

Oh God, how mighty and powerful You are! I look around me in wonder at the mountains and oceans, the fields, deserts, canyons, and plains. You made them all just by speaking them into existence. I gaze up into an infinite breadth of blue. Clouds drift by, slow, undisturbed, and I know that the sky is Yours. You set the sun, the moon, and the stars in place. You know them all by name. When the heavens turn gray and seas go rough, then I feel Your presence. Rain falls. Lightning strikes, and, yet, You protect me. Oh, how strong and loving You are! I see You in birth and also in death. No one but You, God, has the power to give life and to know exactly when it will end. I celebrate each new season and mourn its passing all the while praising You, leaning on You, and loving You. I shout Your name, and I sing Your praises. You alone are my God, the One who always was, always is, and will be forever. Amen.

God's Constant Presence

*Where can I go from your Spirit? Where can I flee from your
presence? If I go up to the heavens, you are there; if I make
my bed in the depths, you are there. If I rise on the wings of
the dawn, if I settle on the far side of the sea, even there your
hand will guide me, your right hand will hold me fast.*

PSALM 139:7–10 NIV

Lord Jesus, sometimes I feel so alone. I start to wonder if there
is anyone who understands me, and I just feel lost and unhappy
with who I am. Would You change those thoughts in me and give
me a new way to think? Give me the desire to get into Your Word
so that You can replace those negative thoughts with Your truth.

I love these verses in the Psalms that promise me that no
matter where I go, You see me and You are with me. What a
huge comfort to my soul! Please change my feelings to match
Your truth. I trust that Your Word is true and that no matter
how I feel, the reality is that You are guiding me and Your hand
is holding mine.

You are a kind and gracious God who sees me as a precious
child—holy and dearly loved. Remind me of Your constant presence in my life. I am so thankful that You know and understand
my wandering heart. Bring me back to the full understanding
that You will never leave or forsake me.

What Wisdom Requires

I keep asking that the God of our Lord Jesus Christ, the glorious
Father, may give you the Spirit of wisdom and revelation.
EPHESIANS 1:17 NIV

Dear Father, life would be so much easier if there were a black-and-white answer to every problem. Or perhaps, if I could just go to an answer bank, submit a question into a machine, and have Your answer for my specific situation printed out for me. . . that would be great. But life's not that simple.

Oh, You gave me guidelines. And there are some black-and-white answers in Your Book. But for most of my questions, I need to figure things out for myself. Except, I don't have to do it *all* by myself. You promised Your wisdom to any who asked.

Lord, wisdom requires me to seek You. Wisdom requires me to ponder and pray and act in faith, even if I'm not sure of the right answer. Wisdom requires me to take time and really think things through, rather than just reacting.

Lord, I want to have Your wisdom. I want You to reveal Your thoughts to me. I want to do things Your way, instead of my own way. I know Your way is much better, by far.

Father, show me Your wisdom today. Reveal Yourself to me. Amen.

God's Life-Giving Light

I pray that your hearts will be flooded with light so that you can understand the confident hope he has given to those he called— his holy people who are his rich and glorious inheritance.

EPHESIANS 1:18 NLT

Father God, as my family and friends join me in studying the truth of Your Word, please fill our hearts with the light of hope. Help us to grasp the realization that the wonderful riches of Your inheritance are Your forgiveness and our redemption through Christ's life-giving sacrifice.

You have blessed us with gifts and a calling to share in Your irrevocable inheritance through Your Son. Our calling is to share Your love wherever we go, using the distinct talents You have bequeathed to us, so that we may teach others about this wonderful inheritance.

We pray in confidence for the unbelievers who cross our paths. We sow the seeds of faith. The Holy Spirit will provide the light and nourishment. For only You know who will respond to the light. Each of us had someone in our pasts who planted those seeds in front of us. Thank You for those believers who prayed for a flood of light to come upon us, bringing us into the hope You have given to us whom You have called.

I pray in the precious name of Jesus Christ, amen.

What Is Unseen

Therefore we do not lose heart. Though outwardly we are wasting away, yet inwardly we are being renewed day by day. For our light and momentary troubles are achieving for us an eternal glory that far outweighs them all. So we fix our eyes not on what is seen, but on what is unseen, since what is seen is temporary, but what is unseen is eternal.
2 CORINTHIANS 4:16–18 NIV

I get so wrapped up in life here on earth. I complain and stress out when troubles come my way. I want success and contentment, and I seek pleasure and entertainment. I want satisfying work, and I try to save and plan so I can retire in comfort. I need Your help, Lord, to keep these things from being my main goal. I need my focus to be on You. I need to be wholly surrendered to You. Help me to want Your will for my life and to serve and work for You alone. Please set my eyes on heaven, reminding me that what is seen here on earth is temporary, and what is unseen is eternal. Keep renewing me from the inside out, comforting me with the fact that as I endure hardship here on earth, You are preparing rewards in heaven that will make all this more than worth it. I trust You for this, Lord, and I long for eternity with You.

Perspective

Give thanks to the LORD, for he is good!
His faithful love endures forever.
PSALM 106:1 NLT

Father, it's been an awful day. It's easy to praise You in the morning. It's my favorite part of the day. Besides, nothing much has happened to disturb me yet. A day like this has jerked me right out of the praise mode.

The dishwasher is broken, and it's leaking through the ceiling into the basement. The repairman said that the part wouldn't be in for a week. The water keeps leaking.

Then I found that the cat had thrown up on the carpet. I had to get on my hands and knees to clean it up.

Later when I walked past the refrigerator, I almost stuck to the floor. Another spill to scrub up. I wet a paper towel, threw it on the spot, and left it to soak.

I could scream! I'd better get out of here and go for a walk.

Oh Lord, what terrible news. A fatal accident happened four blocks away. A speeding car rammed another car that was stopped for the red light. How tragic! I feel numb.

Let me count my blessings. Jesus died for my sins. You love me as Your child. If I'm killed by a speeding car, You'll greet me in heaven. Today's annoyances are nothing in the scope of eternity.

I pray for everyone touched by the wreck—that each would come to know Your amazing love.

Knowledge

*For it is the God who commanded light to shine out of
darkness, who has shown in our hearts to give the light of the
knowledge of the glory of God in the face of Jesus Christ.*

2 Corinthians 4:6 NKJV

All-knowing God, thank You for the knowledge You have revealed to all people: the many intricacies of how the world works and how humans function. I pray for a greater knowledge of these natural things so that my amazement of Your awesomeness keeps growing. When I see unique flowers or understand how a muscle works or learn about ocean currents, let all these facts bring me back to the One who created them. I want to fall on my knees and worship You. Along with the trees and hills that David wrote about, I want to clap and praise You for Your works. They reveal to me more of who You are: a God of order. Even greater than the knowledge of the natural world, I pray for a deeper knowledge of Your law and grace. Guard me against new religions, contradictions, and gossip, which are falsely called knowledge. Bring me each day to study Your promises. Let it be clear in my face and actions that I know Jesus. Use me so that others too will know Him as the great Rescuer and Glory of God. Let me rest at night in the knowledge that You have taught me a little bit more about Yourself and that I listened.

A Heart Built with Wisdom

*Through wisdom is an house builded; and by understanding
it is established: and by knowledge shall the chambers
be filled with all precious and pleasant riches.*

PROVERBS 24:3–4 KJV

God, I could spend every day building my life and my home, but if You're not included, then that life and home will not remain. Wisdom is the principal thing and what I need to build my life upon. You have promised wisdom, if I ask for it, and today I am asking. I need wisdom to build my life, my home, and my family.

Today I open my heart and my home to You. Come in and live with us. I want You to build the house that will not fail. As we come together each day, may Your presence be evident among us. May Your love explode in our hearts for one another and for You.

The material things the world wants and needs fade in comparison to the rich blessings You have for us when You are the center of our world. May my children know You personally, and I pray that my husband and I would put You at the very center of our relationship. We want to make decisions that reflect Your purpose and plan for our lives.

Let the wisdom You give us spill over from our lives and our home into the lives of others. Knit our hearts together with our extended families, friends, and even new acquaintances You bring through our doors. Let wisdom speak in every area of our lives today.

In Spite of Myself

Follow God's example, therefore, as dearly loved children and walk in the way of love, just as Christ loved us and gave himself up for us as a fragrant offering and sacrifice to God.

EPHESIANS 5:1–2 NIV

Lord, this "walking in the way of love" means recognizing that others are different from myself. It means offering grace—Your grace—to everyone around me. Offering grace means knowing that everyone has a story and circumstances that are unique to them. If I take the time to listen to their stories, I may find an understanding beyond my own to offer them more than what I could before.

You love me—despite myself—and because of Your unfathomable love I can offer that to others. I have begun to see that You have much to teach me through others, Lord. Help me listen and learn. It is not my job to fix others, but to pray, and to be shaped and molded into Your image.

A "sacrifice" means a difficult choice. It is offering something that costs me. Your Son sacrificed His life for mine. Can I do less? God, help me to walk this path of love and service, of offering grace when that is a difficult choice. Your Word teaches a way that is not easy, but You promise to be all that we need to be in us. Lord, give me strength and power each day to walk in Your love. Amen.

Hanging Out

*I keep asking that the God of our Lord Jesus Christ,
the glorious Father, may give you the Spirit of wisdom
and revelation, so that you may know him better.*

EPHESIANS 1:17 NIV

Dear Father, I want to know You better. I want to understand Your thoughts. I want Your character to be revealed to me, a little more each day.

If there were a person in my life I wanted to know better, someone I wanted a closer friendship with, there's only one way I could really make that happen. I'd spend more time with that person. I'd engage him or her in conversation. I'd find out what made her laugh and smile, what his interests were, how she interacted with the people around her. Simply put, we'd hang out together.

Lord, You're no different. If I want to know You better, I must spend more time with You. I want to talk to You, not just during my morning or evening prayers, but throughout the day. I want to share each moment with You. Father, I want to watch You interact with the people around me, and join You in Your work.

I want to hang out with You, Lord. Give me wisdom today as You reveal Yourself to me and others. Show me Yourself, so I can grow to be like You. Amen.

Trusting in God's Power When He Is Silent

God has spoken plainly, and I have heard it
many times: power, O God, belongs to you.
PSALM 62:11 NLT

Dear God, forgive me when I forget to trust in You. I know that You are all-powerful and all-knowing and that You love me. But sometimes my mind wanders away from You as I dwell on my problems and the things that I want. That is when I need You the most. You know my trials. You know exactly what I need. Yet when I pray You are silent, and I wonder if You hear me. I know that You are there, God! Your power is beyond my understanding. While I worry and wait, You are there working out the perfect plan to end my trials and give me exactly what I need. Why then, is it hard for me to always trust in You? Why do I run on ahead of You trying to do things on my own? You are the Rock on which I stand. You are my solid ground. So, help me to stand still and turn my thoughts toward You. I do not have to hear from You, again and again, to know that You have my life in Your hands. You have told me many times before. You have everything under control, and You love me. All that You do is perfect. So when You are silent, God, help me to be patient. Help me to trust in Your power and love. Amen.

Morning Praise

Because Your lovingkindness is better than life,
my lips shall praise You.
PSALM 63:3 NKJV

Oh Lord, thank You for catching my eye with pale pink smudges across the sky. I was sure the clouds were too heavy for color this morning. Surprise! I was wrong. I was intent on walking toward my turnaround spot when You snagged my attention. At the hint of color, I stopped to take it all in. Now as I gaze at the pastel strokes, I can't help but praise You. Do the drivers wonder what I'm staring at? Maybe a few will enjoy the fleeting beauty also.

Father, You created me to love early mornings. Sunrises, birdsong, and sparkling spider webs fill me with delight. Thank You for spending time with me. It's so worth the early alarm to meet You on my walks. It's as if we're alone together although traffic rushes by. When I'm thanking and praising You, this world's annoyances and worries drop away. I feel like I'm seated in heavenly places with Jesus (Ephesians 2:6 NIV).

Well, I must move on with my day. As I come back in for a landing, I'm grateful that You're always with me. Not only in the quiet times, but You're with me through the noisy and chaotic ones, too. I love You, Lord. Thank You for Your kind surprise this morning. Your personal gift reveals how much You love me. Help me express Your love to others.

Family Prayer

Unless the LORD builds the house,
the builders labor in vain.

PSALM 127:1 NIV

God of my marriage, thank You for my mate, a gift from You, and a treasure to be valued. Help me see my marriage as a garden to be cultivated and watered and weeded so we will enjoy the fruit of intimate friendship. In my flesh I cannot put others first. Only You can enable me to sacrifice myself joyfully. I'm dependent on You. I also ask You to improve our communication with each other. Help us to express our thoughts and feelings and desires to each other, to share secrets, and work toward mutual goals. Give us acceptance for each other's quirks and preferences. Weed out resentment and enable us to forgive offenses quickly. May we enjoy meeting each other's needs.

Faithful Father, I will never stop giving thanks for the children You have loaned to us. May nothing prevent them from growing in knowledge and wholehearted love for You. Protect them from physical and emotional trauma if it pleases You, but help us to accept unwanted circumstances with grace and submission. Give us wisdom and insight to nurture them by our training and our example to walk with You for life. We need to talk about You when we sit at home, go out on the road, when we lie down and when we get up. Please remind me to create occasions and to take every opportunity You provide today. Amen.

Raised from Death!

I want you to know about the great and mighty power
that God has for us followers. It is the same wonderful
power he used when he raised Christ from death
and let him sit at his right side in heaven.

EPHESIANS 1:19–20 CEV

Heavenly Father, I cherish my risen Savior. His cruel death and triumphant resurrection were part of Your perfect design from the moment Adam and Eve rebelled against You in Eden. You have foretold this divine plan throughout the Bible. Even Abraham believed You would raise the son of his old age from death when he offered Isaac in obedience. You demonstrated Your eternal love when You spared his son at that moment, but not Your own in generations to come. Job proclaimed Your life-giving resolution even in his agony and distress. And the psalmist affirmed his redeemed soul would be rescued from the power of the grave.

Thank You Lord, for the hope You have given me in the knowledge that I, too, have been raised from death to life in Christ's resurrection. Through His prevailing victory over the tomb, I will live on in my own resurrected body long after my corporeal shell passes away. Death has no sting; it holds no victory over me, for I live in Your wonderful promise of eternity with You.

In the name of Him whom You raised, Jesus Christ, I affirm this truth. Amen.

His Calling

*Therefore we also pray always for you that our God would
count you worthy of this calling, and fulfill all the good
pleasure of His goodness and the work of faith with power.*

2 THESSALONIANS 1:11 NKJV

Lord, what are You calling me to? I am called by Your name,
but You also call me *to* something. If You call me far away,
give me strength to be like Abraham whom You called out of
Haran. If You call me to suffer separation from loved ones, let
me be like Joseph. Give me courage, humbleness, and wisdom.
Are You calling me to stand against a certain idol in my life?
Make me like Daniel's three friends who did not give in. Do You
want to use me to convict someone of an unrepentant heart?
Keep me from running or bring me back—like Jonah. Is there
a ministry in which You want me to be involved? Guide me as
You did Timothy, Dorcas, Aquila, and Priscilla. If I am working
in opposition to Your kingdom work, give me a new encounter
with Jesus, like Paul. Let me trust You, even if at the moment
I am unsure of where You are calling me. Speak to me through
the Bible and through prayer. Make me passionate for Jesus'
call for His followers to tell others about God's love. Give me
wisdom to make disciples and to share with others the hope of
His calling, which is peace with God.

Enlightened

I pray that the eyes of your heart may be enlightened in order
that you may know the hope to which he has called you.
EPHESIANS 1:18 NIV

Dear Father, sometimes life feels pretty hopeless. I know I'm supposed to have hope in You, but circumstances cave in on me, piling up on every side, blocking my view. It's hard to see the hope when horrific things are happening all around me.

But Lord, I know I need to be enlightened. I know You want me to see things through Your eyes, through spirit eyes, not through my own human reasoning. When I look at things from Your perspective, my thinking shifts. As I look for You in each situation, *the eyes of my heart are enlightened*, just as Paul wrote.

Even when I can't see You, I can trust You. I can trust Your heart, trust Your love, trust Your perfect wisdom and timing. I can know in my spirit, even when I don't know in my head, that You are working all things together for good for me.

And Father, that gives me hope. That gives me the assurance that this road I'm walking now is only temporary, and You have good, beautiful things in store for my life. Remind me of that, Lord, when I'm ready to give up hope. Help me to see clearly with my heart, even when I can't see with my eyes or my head. Enlighten me. Amen.

Resisting Evil

Submit yourselves, then, to God. Resist the devil, and he will flee from you. Come near to God and he will come near to you. Wash your hands, you sinners, and purify your hearts, you double-minded. Grieve, mourn and wail. Change your laughter to mourning and your joy to gloom. Humble yourselves before the Lord, and he will lift you up.

JAMES 4:7–10 NIV

Heavenly Father, I submit myself to You. Please take control of my thoughts and actions. I ask that You would purify my heart and forgive me for the many times I've sinned against You. I humble myself before You and ask that You lift me out of my pit. I praise You and thank You that You have reconciled my relationship with You once and for all through Christ's finished work on the cross.

You have already won the war! Help me to resist the devil's schemes to lure me into distracting battles here on earth. I know that our enemy tries to get me to stumble in any way he can. And that he prowls around just looking for ways to trip me up. The devil's plan is to render me completely ineffective on this earth. He wants to steal, kill, and destroy me. I pray in Jesus' name that You would help me to resist the enemy's efforts and that You would protect me from his devious plans of attack.

A Light That Shines with Honor

Honor Christ and let him be the Lord of your life.
Always be ready to give an answer when
someone asks you about your hope.
1 PETER 3:15 CEV

Lord, I want to bring You honor in the way that I live my life. I will make mistakes because I am not perfect—but Your grace and mercy give me the strength to get up and try again. May every choice and every decision reflect Your goodness. Help me to be of good reputation and high integrity in all that I do each day.

Like a flashlight that shows you the way to go when you find yourself walking in the forest after dark, I pray that my life will be a light that guides others in the path You have for them. Let me demonstrate Your goodness and Your mercy. I desire to be a picture of Your faithfulness.

It is my heart's desire that others will see my life as something unique and different. May they look into my heart and see the love of God that has been shed abroad in it by Your holy hand. Help me to not be moved by my emotions but by the Holy Spirit. When people look at me, I want them to see You. Let my words be loving and gentle, and my actions reflect a sincere heart to serve You in all I do.

Obedience Instead of Selfishness

*Work hard to show the results of your salvation, obeying God
with deep reverence and fear. For God is working in you,
giving you the desire and the power to do what pleases him.*
PHILIPPIANS 2:12–13 NLT

Father God, I am so grateful that You give me the desire to do
what pleases You! I know the secret depths of my heart, and it
is definitely bent toward my own way. Thank You for working
in me, for helping me become who You created me to be. There
are times for me when obedience is more difficult than others.
Just when I think I've "got it" I am faced with another challenge
from Your Word about how I am to live. Salvation is only the
first step on a long journey.

Help me navigate that path when my desires are selfish, and
when I cannot understand the ways You are working. Changing
and transforming me into Your image can be painful, Lord. The
apostle Paul prays for believers to understand the "incredible
greatness of God's power" (Ephesians 1:19 NLT)—the power that
raised Christ from the dead is the same power working in us!

This is too much for my finite mind to understand, God.
That awesome power is working for my good, not just to change
me but also to help me do what is right, what pleases You. Lord,
remind me that You are doing the work; I only need to cooperate
with You in it. Amen.

Loving God's Word

Thy word is a lamp unto my feet, and a light unto my path.
PSALM 119:105 KJV

I need Your Word every day, Lord. I need it desperately as the lamp and light to guide me in this dark world. Too often, I push time in Your Word to the side, letting all my other plans for the day take precedence, and then I wonder why I feel like I'm stumbling in the dark. *You*, sovereign God, should be my first priority. Help me to crave time with You first thing in the morning so I can start my day out right with eyes fixed on You, with hands and feet and head and heart ready to do Your will.

There are so many things in this life battling for my attention—most of them very demanding. But You won't force me, will You, Lord? You want my *willing*, *devoted* attention. Forgive me when my sin gets in the way of my relationship and communication with You. Thank You that You never give up quietly nudging at my heart to draw me back to You when I stray. I want to be accountable to You and Your Word. Where I need them, please bring fellow believers into my life to help keep me accountable, and for where You have already placed them I am so grateful!

Please help my life be a testimony every single day that Your Word is living and active in me, and it is guiding every step of my way.

Giving Thanks for the Church

So now you Gentiles are no longer strangers and foreigners.
You are citizens along with all of God's holy people. You are
members of God's family. Together, we are his house, built
on the foundation of the apostles and the prophets. And the
cornerstone is Christ Jesus himself. We are carefully joined
together in him, becoming a holy temple for the Lord.

EPHESIANS 2:19–21 NLT

Father, I cannot imagine living without the Church, not only the church that I attend on Sundays but also the world's body of believers in Christ. Together we are one family connected through our Lord and Savior, Jesus Christ. Oh, what a wonderful gift You have given us, this glorious connection through Him. Wherever we travel on earth we are not foreigners, because always there are believers to welcome us. Our family exists in every nation. Even where Christians are persecuted, there they are, standing strong in their faith and worshipping You with love. You have created us to be a welcoming family. Just as Jesus welcomed us, we invite the lost into Your holy temple. We encourage them and adopt them as our brothers and sisters in Christ. Oh, thank You, God, for the Church, and for its Cornerstone, Your Son. He leads us with power and perfect love. Our heritage is strong because of Him. It passes from generation to generation, and His promises never fail. Your family will be together forever, here and also in heaven thanks to Christ's mercy and love! Amen.

Losing It

*Why am I discouraged? Why am I restless? I trust you! And I
will praise you again because you help me, and you are my God.*

PSALM 42:11 CEV

Dear Father, I hate this. I feel so stupid. Once again I'm on the
hunt. I wish that I could call all lost items like I can my cell
phone! That warranty and flash drive must be here somewhere.

This is my third trip through the house. I've raced from
room to room until I'm almost dizzy. Ripping through drawers
and rifling through piles of paper tighten my neck and shoulders.

This time I'll slowly sift through the stacks and in this
drawer. Arggh! The warranty's not here. Not here. How about
here? Am I crazy?

Why can't I focus when I straighten the house? Pay attention to where I put things? Too much whirs in my mind—like a
blender. Everything gets all mushed together.

Oh no! Look at the time. I've got to go. How can I work when
I'm almost worn out? Stop, girl. Take a deep breath.

Okay, Abba, I'm back. The monologue is over. I need Your
help. You know where those things are. I trust You to point me
in the right direction this evening. We've got a history of Your
helping me find things, even contact lenses. Meanwhile, I'll play
praise music while I drive to work. When I focus on You, these
earthly annoyances will fade away.

Thank You for loving me.

Inheritance

*I pray that the eyes of your heart may be enlightened in order
that you may know the hope to which he has called you, the
riches of his glorious inheritance in his holy people.*
EPHESIANS 1:18 NIV

Dear Father, sometimes I forget the true meaning of the word
hope. I find myself hoping it doesn't rain, or hoping my team wins,
or hoping I get a Christmas bonus from my boss. But hope isn't
some feeble wish. The hope that comes from You is a certainty
of Your goodness, an assurance of greater things to come. It's a
firm, unbending belief that my future is glorious.

As Your child, I've already been written into the will. I've
already been given the peace and joy and abundant life promised to Your heirs. But there's more. . .so much more to come,
isn't there?

One day, I'll live with You in Your house. In that place, gold
is so abundant it's poured out like concrete, to build roads. In
Your house, there's a mansion waiting for me. It's not a pretend,
fairy-tale dream. Heaven is a real place, and You have a real
inheritance for Your children.

Until then, Lord, I want to take full advantage of the inheritance I've already received. No matter what my situation, I can
have peace, because peace is already mine. I can have joy, because
You've already granted me full access to Your joy. Remind me
of that, Lord. Amen.

The Well of God's Power Is Full

And what is the exceeding greatness of His power toward us
who believe, according to the working of His mighty power
which He worked in Christ when He raised Him from the dead
and seated Him at His right hand in the heavenly places.

EPHESIANS 1:19–20 NKJV

Almighty, invincible God, You have displayed Your awesome and mighty power in Christ's resurrection, ascension, and exaltation. Your magnificent authority is above and beyond anything we might attempt to imagine. You uphold everything You created by Your powerful word.

Forgive us when we are timid and forget to draw from Your well of power, which You have in store for us. The world of unbelievers sometimes seems too large for us to face. But You are always with us, even when we don't sense Your presence.

Strengthen us, Lord, when we become discouraged, tired, and worn down. Remind us to allow You to work in and through us, according to Your almighty power, as we endeavor to spread Your Gospel. Let us reach for Christ with the same zealous passion as the hordes of people who crushed toward Him, wanting to touch Jesus, hoping His power would heal them.

Thank You, Father, for giving us the Holy Spirit, by which we are able to access Your power to be Your witnesses everywhere we go. I pray this in the name of Jesus. Amen.

Soul Thirst

You satisfy me more than the richest feast.
I will praise you with songs of joy.
Psalm 63:5 nlt

Oh God, You are my God. My soul thirsts for You in a parched and weary land, where nothing quenches my longings except knowing You are with me. Your faithful mercy and compassion are new every day. You lavish me with Your loyal love. Help me to see You in my circumstances, to behold Your power and glory. Your love and kindness are better than life. You satisfy my soul and rejoice my heart. I praise You with my lips and bless You as long as I live. Show me ways to lift up Your name to those who need to see You. May my loved ones know You better by seeing my faith and my love for all Your people. I will never stop thanking You for the family and friends You have given me. I pray they will know Your calling, Your riches, and Your power. For those who don't know You, please enlighten the eyes of their understanding. Help them give up their dependence on other things and run desperately to You.

I lie awake meditating on Your attributes from A to Z. You are my help and strength. Therefore in the shadow of Your wings I rest secure. I cling to You. When I follow You closely, Your strong hand holds me up. May I drink deeply and be refreshed with Your goodness. Amen.

Fullness of Christ

For in Him dwells all the fullness of the Godhead bodily;
and you are complete in Him, who is the head
of all principality and power.
COLOSSIANS 2:9–10 NKJV

Lord, when I look to Jesus what do I see: God, man, Teacher, Friend? Help me to see that Jesus is everything, and all is made whole and perfect in Him. God, give me the knowledge to see Jesus as the fulfillment of all Your promises. I am so thankful that all of Your amazing promises are true. Let me be full of all that is good—of all that is Christ. Fill me with the Truth that is Jesus. Fill me also with the light of Christ, this light which is the real life to men and women. Perfect Teacher, guide me to listen and to put into action what You teach, everything that is beneficial for me. Perfect human, thank You that I can look to You, Jesus for what it means to be truly human. Let me not despair or give in to my weaknesses, or depend on my minimal strength. Empower me to seek the wholeness that is only in Christ, the perfect model. Remind me that I am not deficient or worthless as a human, but that in Jesus, You take away from my character what is sinful and broken. You enrich the traits that are a hidden beauty. Thank You that You make me complete in Christ.

The Lord Is Near

Seek the Lord while you can find him. Call on him now while he is near. Let the wicked change their ways and banish the very thought of doing wrong. Let them turn to the Lord that he may have mercy on them. Yes, turn to our God, for he will forgive generously. "My thoughts are nothing like your thoughts," says the Lord. "And my ways are far beyond anything you could imagine. For just as the heavens are higher than the earth, so my ways are higher than your ways and my thoughts higher than your thoughts."

ISAIAH 55:6–9 NLT

Father, it's hard for me to feel that You are near at times. But I know my feelings can often skew reality. I choose to trust in Your Word that tells me You are close by and that You hear my prayers. I want to seek You with all my heart. Allow me to have a close relationship with You, and give me a deep knowing that You have my life in Your hands.

I pray for friends and family that do not have a true relationship with You. Some don't want anything to do with You, and others have the kind of relationship that is a "form of godliness but denying its power" (2 Timothy 3:5 NKJV). Please soften their hearts and allow them to come humbly to You while You may be found. I ask that You give me wisdom as I interact with these loved ones.

More Grace for Others

*Just as our bodies have many parts and each part has a
special function, so it is with Christ's body. We are many
parts of one body, and we all belong to each other.*
ROMANS 12:4–5 NLT

Thank You, God, for the body of Christ. Sometimes I am disheartened by the things I hear my brothers and sisters in Christ do and say. It is difficult sometimes to walk in love and peace with them. But You desire for us to be one body. Please give me Your grace to navigate the road You have set before us. Help me to walk with them and not stand against them.

Give me the strength to be honest and direct in expressing my feelings and desires. I desire Your wisdom to say what should or should not be said that would bring about Your plan for our lives. We have one God, one faith, and are moving in the same direction.

I desire to be a blessing to everyone I meet—especially those who share my faith. Fill me with the knowledge of Your will, and give me spiritual understanding in how to love those You bring across my path. Fill me with words of encouragement and hope that inspire others to live according to Your Word. Bring us into unity, and give us Your love for one another.

Open My Eyes

*I pray that the eyes of your heart may be enlightened in order
that you may know the hope to which he has called you,
the riches of his glorious inheritance in his holy people.*

EPHESIANS 1:18 NIV

Open my eyes, Lord. Help me to see clearly all that You have for me. It's easy to get distracted by the things around me, things that have little to do with who I am in You.

I look around and see stress, but You've given me peace. I see despair, but You've given me hope. I see myself as powerless to fight against the evil around me, but You've made me powerful.

Father, this world has created a thick film over my eyes. That film keeps Your light from shining through. It keeps me lost, and causes me to bump into things. I'm spiritually blind.

I want to see You. I want to see clearly, the way You see things, but I can't. Not without Your help. Not without Your intervention.

Perform surgery on the eyes of my heart, Lord. Remove the spiritual cataracts that cloud my vision and darken my life. I want a clear view, so Your light, Your love, Your beauty can shine through.

Give me twenty-twenty vision for the spiritual. I want to see every detail of the good things You have for me. Open my eyes, Lord. Amen.

Living in the Body

How good and pleasant it is when
God's people live together in unity!
PSALM 133:1 NIV

Dear Father, thank You for leading my husband and me to this church body. People are welcoming and loving. Gossip is not an issue here. There seems to be an unspoken agreement: no passing on private information unless permitted. We especially are careful not to pass on personal information disguised as prayer requests.

The preaching, teaching, and worship always point us to the Bible, to You. As long as Jesus is recognized as the head of this body, it will function well. I love my two small groups and Sunday school class. Each one is a safe place to take problems and praises. No backstabbing, just trust. And we love one another enough to challenge unbiblical thinking or behavior.

This church is not perfect. At times miscommunication happens and misunderstanding results. Purposeful harm may not be intended, but people are imperfect and get hurt or leave. Satan loves to prey on people's emotions. He lies in wait to whisper deceitful somethings in unguarded minds. I know.

I pray that we, as a body, continually look to You, Lord. That we live in fellowship with one another in Your love, expressing Your love to one another and to visitors. Church should be a pleasant place to go, not one to dread. You placed us in this body, and I am grateful. Help me reach beyond my comfortable circle to visitors or to more isolated members.

Spiritual Wisdom through God's Word

Your teachings are wonderful, and I respect them all.
Understanding your word brings light to the minds of ordinary
people. I honestly want to know everything you teach.

PSALM 119:129–131 CEV

Heavenly Father, whenever I enter my time of Bible study, I thank You for speaking to me through Your Word. Lead me through Your scriptures and enlighten me. Help me to learn Your principles so that I may live in a way that is pleasing to You. Allow Your Word to light my path. The Bible is my map to heaven. When I am weak, it makes me strong. When I am sad, it comforts me. Your Word gives hope to the hopeless and power to the powerless. Its promises fill up my heart with joy. Oh Lord, make me wise in Your truth! Store Your words in my heart, and allow them to fill my mouth with Your praises. Make clear to me the scriptures' hidden meanings. Open my eyes to what I do not understand, for I am Your student, honestly wanting to know everything You teach. Be patient with me as I study. Repeat to me often what I need to know, and give me a firm understanding so that I can share Your wisdom with others. Please quiet my thoughts while we are together in the Word. Inspire me. Take me deeper into understanding more about You and the love that You have for me. In Jesus' name, I pray. Amen.

Modeling God's Love

What if I could speak all languages of humans and of angels? If I did not love others, I would be nothing more than a noisy gong or a clanging cymbal. What if I could prophesy and understand all secrets and all knowledge? And what if I had faith that moved mountains? I would be nothing, unless I loved others. What if I gave away all that I owned and let myself be burned alive? I would gain nothing, unless I loved others. Love is kind and patient, never jealous, boastful, proud, or rude. Love isn't selfish or quick tempered. It doesn't keep a record of wrongs that others do. Love rejoices in the truth, but not in evil. Love is always supportive, loyal, hopeful, and trusting. Love never fails!

1 Corinthians 13:1–8 cev

Heavenly Father, please give me Your love for people. Help me to see them as You do. I get frustrated and impatient with others too quickly. I get tired of helping them with seemingly the same problems over and over. But You love unconditionally. You love tirelessly. You love in all the ways described in this passage of scripture. Thank You for Your amazing love! I desperately need Your help to model it.

If I don't love, then anything I say I'm doing for You is meaningless. Please work in my heart and teach me what Your real love is, and let me share it with others consistently.

The Same Power

*That you may know the hope to which he has called you,
the riches of his glorious inheritance in his holy people,
and his incomparably great power for us who believe.*

EPHESIANS 1:18–19 NIV

Dear Father, sometimes I forget how much power You've given me. Oh, sure. I know I can overcome the little things. But I often think of my faith in You like a little energy shot. . .a tiny boost of caffeine when I'm exhausted. But that doesn't even scratch the surface, does it?

Your power took a dead man and brought Him back to life. Your power took that same man and seated Him at Your right hand. Your power commands the winds, keeps the oceans in check, holds back hell's fury.

Why do I walk around worrying about the future, fretting about this or that, intimidated by little problems that roll into my path? You can make those problems disappear. Or, You can make me strong enough to get through them.

Thank You for Your power, Lord. Remind me today and every day that though I can't move mountains, I have access to the One who can. You live closer than my own heartbeat, and You lean forward to hear my every whisper. I don't have to rely on my own power. . . I simply need to trust You. Amen.

The Right Hand of Majesty

It is the same wonderful power he used when he raised Christ
from death and let him sit at his right side in heaven.
EPHESIANS 1:19–20 CEV

Our sovereign Lord, we congratulate our friends and loved ones, even people who are strangers to us, over and over again for their worldly accomplishments. How many times have we showered them with the words of praise—*awesome*, *magnificent*, or *wonderful*—that we should reserve only for You.

Please forgive us for our foolish tendency to diminish Your awesome greatness. Let us look beyond our own mortal successes and focus on the most magnificent achievement of all times: Christ's wonderful victory over sin and death. As we consider this amazing feat, our short-lived fame loses its luster, fading to a dull finish. Help us to keep our thoughts on You. You proclaimed Christ's royal coronation when You seated Him on Your right side after His ascension. He paid the price for our sin nature once and for all. Taking His seat in that holy place of honor, Jesus proclaimed His work was finished.

Thank You, Father, for establishing the right Hand of Majesty where our Savior now reigns as Your standard of perfection. Let us remember every day to praise Him with our lips, honor Him with our actions and attitudes, and worship Him with our hearts.

Giving Him all praise, honor, and glory, I pray this in Jesus' precious name. Amen.

The Church

And if one member suffers, all the members suffer with it;
or if one member is honored, all the members rejoice with it.
Now you are the body of Christ, and members individually.

1 CORINTHIANS 12:26–27 NKJV

Head of the Church, thank You for uniting Your believers. We praise You for choosing what seems like weak, unlovable, broken people to be the bulk of Your children. Father, I confess that I often forget how important each individual is within Your Church. Forgive me for attributing less value to any one believer. Thank You that even those who seem weak are necessary. Thank You for the metaphor that we are like a body. Give me joy in the knowledge that each member is different and that we need to be working together to spread the hope of Your salvation to others. If I am an eye, let others see Jesus through me; or open my heart to see those around me who are dry and broken. If You wish me to be a mouth, give me boldness to speak the message of the Gospel into their lives. Whichever it is, even if You have me change roles, make me a strong and fruitful member of the body of Christ. If one member suffers, give me a sensitive heart to suffer alongside them. If one of Your children is honored, let me rejoice. Do not give up on Your quarreling children. Apply the balm that is Jesus as the great Reconciler.

Undeserved Gifts

*What do you have that you did not receive? Now if you did
indeed receive it, why do you boast as if you had not received it?*

1 Corinthians 4:7 nkjv

God of my blessings, thank You for the Holy Spirit indwelling
me, illuminating scripture, and revealing You in its pages. You
have enlightened the eyes of my heart to enable me to love You
deeply and follow You closely. I take no credit for wisdom, knowledge, insight, lessons learned, or maturity gained. Everything I
have is an undeserved gift from You. Spiritual fruit is a result of
Your mysterious work in my life, not a reward I have earned or
something I can produce. The truth that You desire me to know
You, that You allow me to scratch the surface in understanding
a quarter molecule of Your attributes—such knowledge is too
wonderful. It is high. I cannot attain to it. Nor can I repay You,
but please accept my gratitude as a sacrifice of praise.

Thank You for all the ways You show up each day. You over-
see my circumstances, create opportunities, prevent calamities,
and empower me to choose what is best. You also suffer with
me and understand my emotions. You waste nothing. Every
hard thing in life draws me closer to You and conforms me
to Christ. Bless the Lord, O my soul. Make me a light to show
others Your goodness and excellence. You alone are worthy of
our praise. Amen.

Don't Get Down

*Why are you cast down, O my soul? And why are you
disquieted within me? Hope in God; for I shall yet
praise Him, the help of my countenance and my God.*

PSALM 43:5 NKJV

Dear God, I don't want to get stuck in pity parties for myself. It's so easy to complain and make a big deal about even the smallest obstacles and frustrations. Not to mention all the big ones! Please help me break that terrible habit and get out of the funks I tend to put myself in. I like things to go according to my plans. I like to set goals and work for them without any hindrance. Yet, it's no secret that life rarely goes exactly according to plan—and getting depressed about it sure won't help matters. Help me to choose a good attitude and put my hope in You no matter what comes my way. It's not easy, but if You help me keep my eyes on You and praise You, I can do it!

I love what the apostle Paul said in his letter to the Romans: "May the God of hope fill you with all joy and peace as you trust in him, so that you may overflow with hope by the power of the Holy Spirit" (Romans 15:13 NIV). You are the God of hope, and when life has me discouraged and anxious, I need You to fill me with Your joy and peace. I trust in You, God! Thank You for being my one true hope!

Set Apart for God

Therefore God exalted him to the highest place and gave him the
name that is above every name, that at the name of Jesus every
knee should bow, in heaven and on earth and under the earth.

PHILIPPIANS 2:9–10 NIV

Jesus, You have been given all authority by the heavenly Father.
Thank You for becoming a man in obedience to the Father's
plan for salvation. I am so thankful that You willingly laid down
Your divine rights, and out of the love for our Father You died
on the cross for my sins. Without Your obedience, I would have
remained separated from God for all eternity—but because of
Your sacrifice I can live forever in heaven.

Just as You did what the Father asked of You, I want to
do likewise. I desire to be set apart and be committed to holy
living. I know that thinking Your thoughts and knowing Your
ways is a big part of being able to follow Your lead. Help me to
read and apply Your Word to my life each day.

Teach me by the Holy Spirit to surrender to the Father's
will in all things. Help me not to justify my actions that go
against God's Word. I want to think Your thoughts and do
what You desire for my life. I choose to be obedient. I desire an
attitude of humility and thankfulness for Your great sacrifice. I
acknowledge You as my Lord and Savior. Today I fully surrender
to Your authority.

My Gracious God

So then, since we have a great High Priest who has entered
heaven, Jesus the Son of God, let us hold firmly to what we
believe. This High Priest of ours understands our weaknesses,
for he faced all of the same testings we do, yet he did not sin.
So let us come boldly to the throne of our gracious God.
There we will receive his mercy, and we will find
grace to help us when we need it most.

HEBREWS 4:14–16 NLT

Lord, sometimes I feel I need to pray like Ezra of the Old Testament: "I am too ashamed and disgraced, my God, to lift up my face to you, because our sins are higher than our heads and our guilt has reached to the heavens" (Ezra 9:6 NIV). I have messed up so many times. The guilt in my heart eats away at me and prevents me from living in freedom and joy. Help me to trust the fact that You convict my heart, but You don't condemn me. You sent Jesus to take away all my guilt and shame so that I can live in joyful freedom while You guide my steps.

You are a gracious God that looks on me with love. You see me through the cross of Christ and I no longer need to feel ashamed in Your presence. Jesus paid the price for my past, present, and future sins, and now I can boldly come into Your presence in a right relationship with You.

Light Their Way

"Let your light so shine before men, that they may see your good works and glorify your Father in heaven."
MATTHEW 5:16 NKJV

Dear Father, I'm amazed that people in this coffee shop seem to be drawn to me. I know it's You in me. It's certainly not my appearance! At 5 a.m. I dare to show up in public without make-up. I usually remember to comb my hair after throwing on my walking clothes. Despite my just-rolled-out-of-bed look, many women and men speak or talk with me. It's definitely You.

Most may not realize that my greeting and smile come from the heart You gave me for people. A few ignore me. One obviously avoids me. However, I've discovered that most people appreciate a smile before beginning their workday. A "Good morning" confirms that someone noticed them. I've learned a few of their stories and offered to pray for them. No one has turned me down. How many here now know Jesus as a Savior? I pray each one will.

Lord, shine through me today. I want everyone to know that I'm Yours and that You're my motivation. If they don't recognize You now, may they someday remember me. I was the gray-haired lady who sat in the coffee shop, Bible and journal open, and greeted them with a smile. An aha moment: *She was a Christian.* Someone You placed in their lives. And may they glorify You, Lord. Never me. Only You.

Love God above All Things

You people aren't faithful to God! Don't you know that if you love the world, you are God's enemies? And if you decide to be a friend of the world, you make yourself an enemy of God.

JAMES 4:4 CEV

Father God, I confess that I have loved worldly things more than I have loved You. The world holds many traps for Your people, and I have fallen into some of them. Time is my enemy. I have spent more time dealing with problems and delights than I have with You. I have spent more time reading for fun and learning than I have reading and studying Your Word. I have worked harder at building good relationships with family, friends, bosses, and coworkers than I have at strengthening my relationship with You. Things get in my way, too, God, things I want, need, and things that I have to do. The enemy is clever. Every day, he comes in disguise. He steals the goodness and love that belong to You.

Father, open my eyes! When I unknowingly turn my attention away from You, speak to my heart. If I don't hear You, speak again. Speak loudly until I hear and obey. Nothing is right if it comes before You in my heart. You are the foundation on which everything else stands. Remind me of that each and every day. And forgive me, Father, for falling into worldly traps. Rescue me from the enemy, and lead me in Your ways. I love You, God. Amen.

Fulfillment

*Praise be to the Lord, to God our Savior, who daily bears
our burdens. Our God is a God who saves; from the
Sovereign LORD comes escape from death.*
PSALM 68:19–20 NIV

My glorious Father, who bears my burdens every day, who protects
me when I don't even realize it. Thank You for the escapes from
death You have given me and my family, Jehovah-*Rapha*, my
Healer. When healing is not Your will, You are my Jehovah-*Jireh*,
my Provider. I am content with You even when I am not comfortable with my circumstances. I can rejoice in You even when I am
filled with sorrow and grief. You comfort me in distress. Although
I seek satisfaction from the people I love and my possessions and
accomplishments, only You can satisfy my heart. Help me to be
filled with Your fullness in every way so that I seek nothing on
earth to fill the holes in my soul. Only You can meet my core needs.
You are enough. Quiet me with Your loving-kindness, the shadow
of Your wings, the river of Your pleasures, Your light and truth.

You are the God of my salvation—past, present, and future.
You have redeemed me forever from sin's penalty and Satan's
power. You are now sanctifying and training me to live in fellowship with You and love You more. And my future salvation
is as secure as Your Word is sure. I will live forever with You.
Oh glorious thought! Amen.

Powerful

And his incomparably great power for us who believe.
That power is the same as the mighty strength he
exerted when he raised Christ from the dead and seated
him at his right hand in the heavenly realms.

EPHESIANS 1:19–20 NIV

Dear Father, wow. Did You really give me the same power You used when You called Christ forth from the dead? Did You really give me the same energy, the same force, the same almighty brawn You hold within Your being?

I guess so. After all, children inherit the traits of their parents. As Your child, I can claim Your qualities. I am powerful because You are powerful.

But what does that mean? What should that look like in my life?

I guess it means I need to quit worrying about stuff. Although I can't always control my circumstances, I have the power to control my reaction to them. I can be peaceful because You are peaceful. I can be calm and loving and kind, even when others aren't, because You are calm and loving and kind. I can display all these qualities without being a doormat. Like You, I can stand firm, flex my spiritual might, and do it with a sweet attitude.

Now that's *power*.

Remind me of that power today, Lord. Remind me that when I rely on You, I don't have to be controlled by any other person or circumstance. I'm powerful, because I am Yours. Amen.

Now and Forever

*Far above all principality and power and might and
dominion, and every name that is named, not only
in this age but also in that which is to come.*

EPHESIANS 1:21 NKJV

Eternal Father, You appeared to the world in ancient times in the form of the perfect man of Jesus. You bless us in the present age by appearing through Your holy scriptures.

You have given us a history filled with promises of hope for our future. Yet we tend to focus on the present. We often neglect our reading of the testimonies described in the Bible of man's constant battle with sin and Your abiding forgiveness. We sometimes dismiss our eternal future, selfishly contemplating our next few earthly moments. Help us to remember that our existence on earth is only for a moment. Our hope is in eternity.

Let us not be like the tares that are gathered up and burned at the end of this age, but help us to use what talents You have generously bestowed upon us during this life to further spread the Gospel of our Savior.

We give thanks for the abundant resources of Your blessings to us in Christ Jesus. Let us live in a manner today that honors You so that we may provide a true representation of Your grace for those who follow us in the future.

I pray this in the name of Jesus Christ, who was and is and is to come—the Alpha and the Omega. Amen.

Your Bounty

Every good gift and every perfect gift is from above,
and comes down from the Father of lights.

JAMES 1:17 NKJV

Bless the Lord, Oh my soul. All that is within me blesses Your holy name. You have been bountiful to me. You forgive and redeem me. You crown me with Your loyal love and kindness so that I am satisfied in You. I recall all Your benefits, and it renews and refreshes me. Praise the Lord, O my soul. You are the God of my daily benefits. Help me not to doubt You or to think You are not enough.

Forgive me for believing I'm entitled to Your blessings. And for feeling slighted when You withhold what I have begged You for, while others seem to get it without striving. I'm sorry for coveting and comparing and complaining. I deserve nothing from You. Everything I have is a bonus—every breath, every hair, every relationship, every ability and accomplishment—it all belongs to You. You are the Source of all my gifts, and You deserve all my appreciation. Yours is the glory. Train my focus away from what I don't have, what I used to have, what I could have, to make me thankful for what I do have because of Your generous grace. May I never cease giving thanks or being grateful for the hope of Your calling, the riches of Your glory, and the greatness of Your power. Bless the Lord, Oh my soul. Amen.

Needing Wisdom

If you need wisdom, ask our generous God, and he will give it to you. He will not rebuke you for asking. But when you ask him, be sure that your faith is in God alone. Do not waver, for a person with divided loyalty is as unsettled as a wave of the sea that is blown and tossed by the wind. Such people should not expect to receive anything from the Lord. Their loyalty is divided between God and the world, and they are unstable in everything they do.

JAMES 1:5–8 NLT

Dear God, I forget to ask You for wisdom sometimes, and it is my huge loss. Your Word promises You are generous and will give wisdom to anyone who asks for it. I need Your wisdom in every aspect of my life. Before making decisions, help me to consider Your will and request Your wisdom. Help me to make good choices in all that I do and say, striving for a lifestyle that honors You.

And when I've asked for wisdom, please make me confident that You will follow through. You will give it to me and guide me. I don't want to be wishy-washy or insecure in my faith, so please help me not to doubt You.

I can't fully trust in anything or anyone but You, God, because the things of this fallen world will fail me. But You will never fail me—thank You for that! Anchor me solidly in my faith in You, and please fill me generously with Your wisdom.

Christ's Intercession

*Seeing then that we have a great High Priest who has
passed through the heavens, Jesus the Son of God, let us
hold fast our confession. For we do not have a High Priest
who cannot sympathize with our weaknesses, but was
in all points tempted as we are, yet without sin. Let us
therefore come boldly to the throne of grace, that we may
obtain mercy and find grace to help in time of need.*

HEBREWS 4:14–16 NKJV

God on High, I praise You for being the One who remains holy
and pure. You see how I am filled with brokenness. How can I
ever hope to be near to You? Purge me of my sins and I will be
clean; wash me and I will be whiter than snow. Thank You that
even though You require perfect goodness, You have given me
the One who is good—Jesus, God incarnate. Great intercessor,
I am weak. Remind me that Jesus also felt weak in the garden.
When I fight bitterly against temptation, let me cling to the
strength of Jesus, who did not give in to Satan's lies. If I do
fall, give me a contrite heart to boldly come before Your throne
and ask forgiveness. Great High Priest, thank You that You
sacrificed Yourself for me. Amazing love, You pursued me to
death so that I may know life to the fullest followed by eternity
with God. Let me give my forever Priest a positive and fruitful
account to present to God.

To Reflect Him More

"If you had known Me, you would have known My Father also;
and from now on you know Him and have seen Him."

JOHN 14:7 NKJV

God, I want to know You more. You are the One I serve; the
One I love. You saved me and gave me everything. I don't have
to go through life alone, wondering about why I am here. I look
to the Bible and discover the life of Jesus. As I come to know
Him—His character and nature—I come to know You even more.

As I study the lives of the men and women in the Bible and
the choices they made, I realize I can trust You to keep Your
promises. I want to be a doer of Your Word. Help me to keep
Your principles first in my heart. May my actions and decisions
reflect who You are.

Thank You for time in prayer where You speak to my heart
and give me instruction and peace. I pray to be more Spirit-led
as I learn to follow Your voice. Thank You for Your Holy Spirit
that speaks to my spirit and leads me. I am determined to listen
and act on the things that You lead me to do and say.

Thank You for Your peace that brings understanding to my
heart and allows me to walk by faith each day. I want to know
You more. Help me to grow each day closer to You!

Who's on First?

I bow my knees to the Father of our Lord Jesus Christ,
from whom the whole family in heaven and earth is named.
EPHESIANS 3:14–15 NKJV

Creator God, thank You for the myriad of ways You reveal Yourself. In the variety and complexity of nature, in the organized harmony of the universe, and through Your written Word, which provides everything necessary for life and godliness. All heaven worships You. Someday everyone who has ever existed will bow to you. You alone are worthy of all worship. As vast and almighty and infinite as You are, yet You have enlightened the eyes of my heart to give me a growing relationship with You. I—so unworthy. I take no credit for my awards and accomplishments, my abilities and talents. Even though I plant and water and weed, You cause the fruit to form in my life to nourish others. My only response is awe and humble worship.

Sovereign Lord Jesus, You are Number One over all the universe and all creation. You are Head of the Church. I am humbled to be a member of that Church Universal, Your Body. How unworthy I am to be a saint. Please help me remember to keep You Number One in my life, as my Head. I gladly surrender to all You have planned for me. I am yoked with You, my ministry partner. Help me submit to You today and let You do all the pulling. I bow to You. Amen.

Child of the King

He raised Christ from the dead and seated him at his right
hand in the heavenly realms, far above all rule and authority,
power and dominion, and every name that is invoked,
not only in the present age but also in the one to come.

EPHESIANS 1:20–21 NIV

Dear Father, it's hard for me to comprehend who I am in You. Yes, I'm Yours. But often, I live like a peasant when I should be living like royalty. You rule over everything, and I'm Your child.

Lord, Your Son has been placed above every authority, every power, every dominion. . .and I'm a joint heir with Christ. I'm Your adopted child, which makes me part of the royal family.

Just as an earthly prince or princess wouldn't beg in the streets or be bullied by lowlifes, I don't have to be bullied by ungodly people or circumstances. I can go to You, my Father, and Christ, my Brother, and take control of any situation. My standing holds prestige. My placement in Your family comes with privilege.

When Satan tries to intimidate me, remind me who I am. When I feel oppressed by circumstances, call to mind Your strength. Send Your Holy Spirit to advise me how to use my placement in Your family. I know You don't want me living like a peasant anymore. You want me to live like a child of the King. Amen.

Praising God's Love

*For I am convinced that neither death nor life,
neither angels nor demons, neither the present nor
the future, nor any powers, neither height nor depth,
nor anything else in all creation, will be able to separate
us from the love of God that is in Christ Jesus our Lord.*

ROMANS 8:38–39 NIV

Oh God, how great Your love is! Your love for me is so powerful that nothing can stop or weaken it. It reaches beyond all circumstances. Nothing on earth, past, present, or future can take it away. You created me out of love. Your love formed me in my mother's womb. It gave me life! You love me unconditionally. When I disobey You, whenever I sin, You forgive and correct me with love. Your love desires nothing but goodness for me, and Your love leads me through the valleys. You love me so much that You sent Jesus to save me from death. He gave His life, all that He could give, because You knew that I would continue to disappoint You by sinning. Out of love, You sent Jesus so that I could be forgiven and live forever with You in heaven. Oh Father, how great Your love is! It warms my heart and brightens my days. It motivates me to love others the way that You love me—faithfully, forgivingly, and unconditionally. I praise You, God, because You are good. Your love endures forever. Thank You, God, for Your infinite love! Amen.

Bringing My Feelings to God

Have mercy on me, O God, have mercy! I look to you for
protection. I will hide beneath the shadow of your wings until
the danger passes by. I cry out to God Most High, to God who
will fulfill his purpose for me. He will send help from heaven
to rescue me, disgracing those who hound me. My God will
send forth his unfailing love and faithfulness.

PSALM 57:1–3 NLT

Thank You that we can call on You and share all of our thoughts
with You at all times. I know You want me to bring all of my
worries and cares to You instead of gossiping with someone
else. When I feel hounded and annoyed by others, please help
me to keep calm and bring my feelings to You alone. I pray as
David prayed: "Create in me a clean heart, O God. Renew a
loyal spirit within me. Do not banish me from your presence,
and don't take your Holy Spirit from me. Restore to me the joy
of your salvation, and make me willing to obey you" (Psalm
51:10–12 NLT).

I surely don't deserve the mercy that You offer to me, but
I beg it of You. I fail too often and choose my way instead of
Yours. Forgive me for my sins of pride and selfishness. My ego
gets in the way too many times to count. Bring these sins and
flaws of mine to my attention quickly, Lord, so I can be made
right with You again.

Being Still

Be still, and know that I am God; I will be exalted
among the nations, I will be exalted in the earth!
PSALM 46:10 NKJV

Oh Lord, You are my refuge and strength, my fortress and strong tower, my defender and deliverer. Please fight my battles today while I stop struggling and wait on You. Take my fears and troubles. May I not be overcome by the conflicts around me, the pressures on me, and the wars within me. Give me peace in the midst of whatever chaos I encounter today, and help me to handle it all by depending on You for wisdom and understanding.

God of grace and glory, I grieve over this country's conflicts and over wars throughout the world. Starving people, persecuted Christians, babies being killed, children being hurt and victimized. Meet the needs of the oppressed. Give them grace and endurance, help and hope. Show me how to do my part to encourage the grieving and strengthen the weak. Break the bow and spear and be exalted by all nations, as You promised. Your Word says to be still—to cease striving—and know that You are the one true God who fights for us. Your power exceeds all greatness. You are almighty over everything, even Satan. Help me remember he is a defeated enemy who has no power over me. I exalt You. Be exalted in the world. May Your will be done on earth as it is in heaven. Amen.

Name above All Names

Far above all principality and power and might and
dominion, and every name that is named, not only
in this age but also in that which is to come.
EPHESIANS 1:21 NKJV

Our hallowed Father, You have given exclusive names to the
angelic beings in the heavens, as well as every star and planet
in the vast universe. Even all the animals that roam the earth
and all the birds in the air have names. Each of the countries
is designated by an appropriate name, as are the mountains,
waterways, and canyons on this beautiful earth. Yet You have
exalted our blessed Savior above all the names of Your creation.
No name is higher than the one which You have entrusted to our
Lord, Jesus Christ. It is the name above every name; a name only
You know and will reveal to us believers in the future.

Lord, please help us to fathom the significance of so great
an exaltation. Let us lift Christ up in our own lives, offering
Him praise and honor, giving Him a place in our hearts high
above anything and everything that is precious to us, even our
own names.

Thank You, gracious God, for this glorious confirmation of
the magnitude of our Savior. I pray this in the most excellent
name of my wonderful Savior, Jesus Christ. Amen.

Joy in the Lord

Always be full of joy in the Lord. I say it again—rejoice!
PHILIPPIANS 4:4 NLT

Dear Abba, thank You for letting me know the answer to my prayer for a friend. I hadn't seen her since she returned from her trip. I missed her at the coffee shop again this morning. Or so I thought.

After my walk, I took a minute to peer in the shop's big windows. There she was standing in line! I hurried inside. On a Sunday morning neither of us had much time. Yet I had to ask about her and her husband's Colorado trip. She summed it up in one delicious word, "Refreshing!"

My heart leaped with joy! She'd specifically asked me to pray for refreshment. Her request returned to my mind every day that they were gone. And You answered gloriously. I grinned throughout her brief description of their wonderful escape. Did I glow with delight and gratitude?

Father, once again You confirmed Your listening ear and loving heart. Your Holy Spirit reminded me to pray and guided me. I've learned how much You love individuals and care about their needs. To be used by God Almighty to affect another person's life is exquisite. I suppose my feet stayed on the ground as I returned to my car. But I felt like I floated along in the breeze of Your presence. All of this was provided through the blood of Jesus. Unbelievers just don't know what they're missing.

Handicapped

And God placed all things under his feet and appointed him
to be head over everything for the church, which is his body.

EPHESIANS 1:22–23 NIV

Dear Father, my head is pretty important. Though it doesn't take up much space compared to the rest of me, it's the most important part. It's the control center. I could live without a toe or a finger, or even without an arm or a leg. I could even live without a kidney. But without my head, I'm nothing.

If there's a malfunction, and my body doesn't do what my head tells it to, I'm going to have problems. If my head says to walk and my feet won't listen, I'll be crippled. If my head tells my hands to write, and they won't follow orders, I'll be handicapped. The only way I can function at my best is if my body does what my head commands.

My spirit is no different, Lord. You are my head, my boss, my commander in chief. At times I don't obey You. When that happens, I handicap myself. I don't know why I try to go my own way; I know You love me and only want the best for me. You'll never direct me to anything that's not for my ultimate good. Remind me to trust You, to follow You, and to obey Your orders. When I do, I know I'll be at my best. Amen.

Resurrection

Now if we died with Christ, we believe that we shall also live with Him, knowing that Christ, having been raised from the dead, dies no more. Death no longer has dominion over Him.

ROMANS 6:8–9 NKJV

Giver of life, on that first Passover the blood of the lamb saved Your people from death. But sin remained, and through it the power of death. Only the perfect Lamb, whose blood mingled with the hyssop branch on the cross, can save me. Thank You that His death did not end in the grave but in salvation for all. Christ overcame death so that I, in Jesus, can say, "Where is your sting, Death?" Thank You that the death You call us to produces life. Just as Jesus died so I could live, help me to die to sin. Energize me with the strength of Your Spirit to bury my sinful nature daily—my unclean thoughts, unkind words, apathetic attitude. In baptism, I declare You to be the One who is the life of men and women and I bury my old, unrepentant self. Empower me to see my physical death not as a point of sorrow, but as an anxious passing to the longed-for resurrection and beautiful fellowship in heaven. All of this is done through death to show me that the wisdom of humans is foolishness to God. Guard me so that I who died to sin will no longer live captive to my weaknesses.

Unity of Heart

That we henceforth be no more children, tossed to and fro,
and carried about with every wind of doctrine, by the sleight
of men, and cunning craftiness, whereby they lie in wait to
deceive; but speaking the truth in love, may grow up into
him in all things, which is the head, even Christ.

EPHESIANS 4:14–15 KJV

Lord, I am a part of Your body and I represent You in all that I say and do. I know from the Bible that it is Your desire for believers to work together and bless one another. The words I speak and that others speak to me are important to both my relationship with You and with them.

When others speak to me, let me hear what You would have me hear. Let me be slow to anger and full of mercy and grace. And if the words of others hurt or condemn, then help me to let go of those words quickly and forgive the one who said them. Show me how to guard my heart from those things I don't need to hear.

I pray my words are truth and life to all who hear them. Help me by Your Holy Spirit to speak words that bring good things into people's lives. When I need to say something that will be difficult for others to hear, please give me the right words that will speak directly into the heart of the hearer and bring about Your purpose and desire for his or her life.

Guide Me in Wisdom

If you need wisdom, ask our generous God, and he will give it to you. He will not rebuke you for asking. But when you ask him, be sure that your faith is in God alone. Do not waver, for a person with divided loyalty is as unsettled as a wave of the sea that is blown and tossed by the wind. Such people should not expect to receive anything from the Lord. Their loyalty is divided between God and the world, and they are unstable in everything they do.

JAMES 1:5–8 NLT

Lord, I have come to You with this same request for wisdom in the past. Thank You for being so generous with me. Thank You for allowing me to come into Your presence because of what Jesus Christ did for me on the cross. I know that You alone are the answer to all my questions and needs. You see all and know all. I trust that You alone are sovereign. You have everything planned out according to Your great will.

Please help me not to doubt Your plans for me, Lord. Especially when it looks like what is unfolding before me doesn't match up with what I planned. I do want Your will in my life, Father. I want to be known and to be used by You for Your greater purposes. I trust You to lead and guide me in wisdom.

No Need for Pity

If Christ has not been raised, then your faith is useless and you are still guilty of your sins. In that case, all who have died believing in Christ are lost! And if our hope in Christ is only for this life, we are more to be pitied than anyone in the world. But in fact, Christ has been raised from the dead.

1 CORINTHIANS 15:17–20 NLT

Jesus, thank You for Your resurrection! I praise You that You are worthy of my faith because You are, in fact, risen! You overcame death, and because of that, You offer us hope for eternal life too. There are many religions with many prophets and leaders with claims to providing the way to God and heaven, but *You* are the one true Source of real hope. Believing in You is the one true religion. You are the Way, the Truth, and the Life, and no one comes to the Father except through You. Thank You that You have already done the work that is required to be a follower of You. There are no works to be done to receive Your salvation; it's simply a matter of accepting the gift You offer by grace.

Thank You, that as a follower of You, I am *not* to be pitied more than all others. Help me to share the real and only hope of Your resurrection in unapologetic but always loving ways.

When I Don't Understand

May the God of hope fill you with all joy and peace
as you trust in him, so that you may overflow
with hope by the power of the Holy Spirit.

ROMANS 15:13 NIV

Lord, so much is beyond my understanding. I ask, Why do bad things happen to good people? Why do the evil prosper? Why do some suffer from illnesses while others are cured? You are a good and loving God. I believe that with all my heart. When I pray, I know that You hear me. Yet sometimes I feel disappointed when You don't answer my prayers in the way that I want. I don't understand why You allow evil to roam the earth. But, Lord, there is one thing that I do know—You understand. You know the answers to all my questions. Your answers are hidden from me now, but one day I will know. You will enlighten me with Your wisdom and truth. My hope and trust are in You. When I see evil reign and I ask why, I know that You will send Your Holy Spirit to soothe me and bring me joy and peace. When Your answers are too wise for my understanding, I know that the power of Your Holy Spirit will give me hope. Oh God, how grateful I am that You are in control. I know that in the end all evil will cease and everything on earth and in heaven will exist in harmony with You. Amen.

Surrender

The LORD is like a father to his children,
tender and compassionate to those who fear him.
PSALM 103:13 NLT

Abba, Father, how long? Oh Lord, how long will I have this sorrow in my heart? This daily misery? How long will overwhelming grief be constantly on my mind? Hear me, O Lord. You are my God. Turn and answer me. Restore the sparkle to my eyes, and defeat my emotional enemies. I trust in Your unfailing love. Let me rejoice in Your deliverance. Guard my heart from resentment and rage, bitterness and blame. May this cup pass from me, or else give me the willpower to drink it in fellowship with You. You are the God who sees and hears. You understand my sorrow and struggle, and You know how weak I am. You remember that I am only dust. Since You have called me to bear this burden, I wait on You for spiritual wisdom to have confident hope in Your purposes. My times are in Your hand—my beginning and end and everything in between.

Father God, I surrender all, not because I'm backed against a wall. Life's too hard to bear it apart from Your control, so take me—body, mind, and soul. On You I fall. Keep me submitted to Your will and committed to Your Word. Then I will not rebel against Your ways. You know what You're doing in my life, and that means I don't have to. Amen.

Any Circumstance

He heals the brokenhearted and bandages their wounds.
He counts the stars and calls them all by name. How great
is our Lord! His power is absolute! His understanding
is beyond comprehension!

PSALM 147:3–5 NLT

Lord, I confess that I am full of questions longing to be answered. There is so much I don't understand. I battle doubts and fear; I see suffering and evil and ask, "Why?" I listen for Your voice and hear only silence. But You are neither hard of hearing nor lacking in compassion! The psalmist tells us that Your arm can save, that Your power is absolute, and that we cannot fully comprehend You.

Father, I am thankful that You are beyond the ability of my finite mind to understand and comprehend. Your majesty, might, holiness, righteousness, grace, mercy, love. . .because of these I can put my trust in You. Your power surpasses anything man-made. I know that You can take any circumstance and make good come from it. I can count on You to see me through any difficulty, to hold my hand when I am hurting, and to guide my path through all uncertainties. Help me Lord, to lean on Your strength and ability to save, not my own. "But when I am afraid, I will put my trust in you" (Psalm 56:3 NLT).

Lord, I cry with the psalmist, "Give me understanding and I will obey your instructions; I will put them into practice with all my heart" (Psalm 119:34 NLT). Amen.

Everlasting Kingdom

There Christ rules over all forces, authorities, powers,
and rulers. He rules over all beings in this world and
will rule in the future world as well. God has put all
things under the power of Christ, and for the good of
the church he has made him the head of everything.

EPHESIANS 1:21–22 CEV

Our Father in heaven, the governments in this world give all the appearances of strength and dominance. It's easy for us to forget, when we hear of leaders who abuse their power, that You created every throne and every dominion. You set rulers in their positions of authority. Some as a blessing for us, and others as punishment for turning away from You.

When we try to be kings in our own little corners of the world, we often pay the price of making our situations worse. Then You call us back, reminding us to give our lives back to You. Even when Your resolution isn't the one we prefer at that moment, we usually see in hindsight that Your solution was perfect.

The peace of Christ could rule, mediate, or resolve every situation of our lives, if only we would allow it. As Christ rules over all kingdoms and nations, I pray that we remember to let Him rule in our hearts and minds.

Thank You, Father, for Your gracious kingdom!

I pray this in the name of our righteous and loving King, Jesus Christ, whose kingdom is everlasting. Amen.

God's Handiwork

Come, let us sing for joy to the LORD; let us shout aloud to the Rock of our salvation. Let us come before him with thanksgiving and extol him with music and song. For the LORD is the great God, the great King above all gods. In his hand are the depths of the earth, and the mountain peaks belong to him. The sea is his, for he made it, and his hands formed the dry land. Come, let us bow down in worship, let us kneel before the LORD our Maker; for he is our God and we are the people of his pasture, the flock under his care.

PSALM 95:1–7 NIV

Father, I look out over all You have made and I am so thankful that You show Yourself to me daily in real, tangible ways. I see Your handiwork in the trees and the flowers, the painted skies and natural wonders. I see it in the little children and their joy at discovering Your creation. As each of us takes part in this beautiful world You created, let us come before You in all praise and honor. Let us give You credit for the amazing works You have accomplished.

The joy You've placed in my heart makes me want to sing and shout aloud to all the earth. Thank You for my church where I have the ability to sing and proclaim Your name out loud with fellow believers. You are great, Oh Lord. Thank You for all You have done.

In His Name

Whatever you say or do should be done in the name of the Lord
Jesus, as you give thanks to God the Father because of him.
COLOSSIANS 3:17 CEV

Dear Father, my job is getting hard to take. This entry-level work requires so little skill. I feel like a high school kid. It's a difficult transition from leader to underling. I know I left the leadership position by choice years ago. But it's hard, God. Whine, whine, whine.

Do I sound like a rebellious adolescent? My teenage children and my students aggravated me whenever they continuously complained. After a while their cranky words grated on me like a drippy faucet. Um, am I annoying You?

Your Word says that I should do everything in the name of Jesus. Everything. Not just prayer and Bible study. Even menial jobs. Hmm. Maybe I need an attitude adjustment. To work in His name sheds new light on my position and on my stinky disposition. Ick!

Father, I'm sorry for my petulant attitude. Thank You for my job. You provided it when my husband and I needed a little extra income. I remember warm excitement when the job was offered. Back then I was all smiles and full of praise. Please remind and help me to work well. I don't want to reflect badly on my Lord.

Abba, I'm grateful that Jesus took my every sin on the cross, including my puffed-up pride. His sacrifice means heaven to me.

Hands and Feet

*The church, which is his body, the fullness
of him who fills everything in every way.*
EPHESIANS 1:22–23 NIV

Dear Father, it's easy to think of You as distant. Because I can't see You, it seems at times like You're not really here. When I don't have a physical representation of Your love, I feel alone.

But that's not the way it's supposed to be, is it, Lord? You designed the Church to be Your body. You designed the Church to give hugs to the lonely, to fix meals for the hungry, to run errands for the invalid.

The Church. . .that's me, isn't it? I'm a part of Your Church. That means I'm a part of Your body. It's my job to be Your hands and feet and heart on this earth.

Father, I've not always done a good job of being Your flesh-and-blood representation. I become absorbed in my own world, my own needs, and I forget to offer myself to others. Please forgive me, and help me love the people You've placed around me in real, flesh-and-blood, up-close-and-personal ways.

Show me practical things I can do, whether it's a hug or a smile or a meal. Perhaps I can make a phone call to let someone know they matter, or wheel their trash can to the curb. The possibilities are endless.

Show me, Lord. Help me. I want to be Your hands and feet in this world. Amen.

That Same Power Lives in Me

*"But God set him free from death and raised him to life.
Death could not hold him in its power."*

ACTS 2:24 CEV

Heavenly Father, it is so overwhelming sometimes for me to try to comprehend Your power, and the truth that Your power resides in me. Then I think about Romans 8:11, which says the same spirit that raised Christ from the dead lives in me. Your ultimate power that created the world, brought the first man and woman to life, and reached into the depths of hell in order to bring back Jesus from the dead, lives in me! I accept that truth with faith in Your promises today.

I want to experience my life each day on Your terms and not on mine. Sometimes I fall captive to sin, but as I repent and allow You to move in my life, I can expect no less power in my life than the power that flowed through Jesus on His resurrection day.

Father, continue each and every day to live and breathe life into me just as You did in Jesus when He walked this earth. I have a great expectation for You to continually redeem me from the dead life and bring me into continual life in You!

From God with Love

Take delight in the Lord, and he will
give you the desires of your heart.
PSALM 37:4 NIV

Dear Lord, thank You for a morning with You. During my quiet time, I contemplated my inheritance because of Jesus. He paid for all my sins, and You're not mad at me. Even when I mess up. His sacrifice assures me of a bright forever.

Later, our Sunday worship reminded me of who You are: the only One worthy of praise. Next, the sermon challenged me to be real with You and get rid of distractions. In addition, I always enjoy being in fellowship with my church family.

My focus has been on You all morning. I chatted with two or three others before leaving church. My smile seems firmly planted on my face, as if it will never disappear. I know that's not true, but for now I bask in Your love. Lord, I love You so much.

Aww. I see it! A monarch is directly over my open sunroof, gliding on orange-and-black wings backlit by the sun. Well, there goes another one. I almost missed it but glanced up before pulling from my parking space. Thank You, Father! How do those delicate little things fly all the way to Mexico for the winter? Because You designed them to!

Sighting monarchs through an open sunroof—a happy coincidence? Nope. It's a desire of my heart, a gift from my Abba. I'm so loved. Thank You.

Blessings

And what is the exceeding greatness of His power toward us who believe, according to the working of His mighty power.

EPHESIANS 1:19 NKJV

Fount of every blessing, thank You for the beautiful outpouring of Your mysterious ways on those who believe in You. I know that even this faith is from You, that it is the work of the Holy Spirit in my heart. Thank You that out of Your power comes all that is good. You are able to use even the awful sufferings in my life to bring unimaginable blessings. You redeem, rejuvenate, and reconcile. Let me remember that even Your chastisement is a blessing because it brings me back to the foundation of my belief—You are God and I was made to enjoy You forever. Your Word—both Son and scripture—are the reason and source of my belief. Guide me to daily drench myself in the blessings that flow from Your Word. Take the empty jars in my heart and mind and fill them with the life-giving water of Jesus, like You did with the Samaritan woman at the well. Lord, I believe You did great things. But I often forget that You are doing amazing things now. Jesus said that those who did not see all His miracles, yet still believed, are blessed. Let me truly be one of these people. Open my eyes to see Your blessings now and to let Your power work in me.

Giving Thanks for Jesus

And we know that the Son of God has come, and he has
given us understanding so that we can know the true God.
And now we live in fellowship with the true God because
we live in fellowship with his Son, Jesus Christ. He is
the only true God, and he is eternal life.

1 JOHN 5:20 NLT

Dear God, what an amazing gift You gave us in our Lord, Jesus Christ! The prophets foretold His coming. Through them You prepared the world for Your advent. You came in flesh as the Son. You came as Jesus, the child, born in humble surroundings but with such power that angels arrived to slay the darkness. Your star revealed that light had come into the world. Christ lived as He was born, in humility, yet with all of Your power and strength. He healed the sick, walked on water, and performed miracles that only You can do. Each word He spoke had purpose and meaning. His words, Your words, transcend time. We read them in our Bibles and trust in their wisdom. Oh thank You, God, for Jesus!—God in skin, One like us, speaking to us, living with us, teaching us, and loving us as only You can love. He saved us by Your grace. He washed away our sin and gave us the promise of eternal life. He is with us now and forever. Oh God, thank You so much for Jesus. Thank You for Your wonderful gift! Amen.

Rejoice, Pray, and Give Thanks

Rejoice always, pray continually, give thanks in all circumstances;
for this is God's will for you in Christ Jesus. Do not quench the
Spirit. Do not treat prophecies with contempt but test them
all; hold on to what is good, reject every kind of evil. May
God himself, the God of peace, sanctify you through and
through. May your whole spirit, soul and body be kept
blameless at the coming of our Lord Jesus Christ. The
one who calls you is faithful, and he will do it.

1 THESSALONIANS 5:16–24 NIV

Heavenly Father, there are definitely times when I do not feel like giving thanks. Especially when life seems overwhelming. Please forgive me for the stress and anxiety that I allow to consume me. I ask that You carry my burdens and that You would give me the strength and ability to be thankful in every circumstance.

Remind me of Your presence in my life at all times, not just in times of trouble. I know You want to share all of life with me. Yes, You're there for me in hard times, but You want to rejoice with me in good times, too. You are a good and faithful God who offers me peace in anything I face. I praise You for Your faithful, unfailing love. Give me the strength and willingness to hold on to all that is good in my life and to reject any evil that comes my way.

Delighting in Differences

*There are different kinds of spiritual gifts, but they all come
from the same Spirit. There are different ways to serve the same
Lord, and we can each do different things. Yet the same God
works in all of us and helps us in everything we do. The Spirit
has given each of us a special way of serving others.*

1 CORINTHIANS 12:4–7 CEV

Dear Lord, help me to love the diversity among Your people and the diversity among the gifts You have given us. I get self-centered too often and expect that every fellow Christian should be more like me, but that's not right at all! Help me not to compare and contrast my strengths and weaknesses with others. I sometimes judge and criticize. I sometimes become jealous over what I can't do well and prideful over what I can. Instead, please help me to only compare myself with You. I want to celebrate the fact that You have given us all different gifts and we can use them to serve You and serve others in very different ways. I can't possibly know how You use each different person to further Your kingdom, but I praise You that You do!

Please remove all pride and jealousy from me, and help me focus on wanting to be like You, Jesus, not like anyone else. Help me to discover and develop my own spiritual gifts with the right attitude. I want to use them for Your glory.

Sweet Anointed Feet

*And hath put all things under his feet, and gave
him to be the head over all things to the church.*

EPHESIANS 1:22 KJV

Heavenly Father, we often balk at the notion of being considered someone else's lowly footstool. We take offense at people who figuratively wipe their muddy shoes on us, using our backs as a springboard for their own worldly successes.

Please help us to see there is a huge difference between being under the oppressive feet of another person, whose thoughtless actions are for selfish gain, and being under the divine feet of Christ, where we find a calming shelter from the world's negative influences. Give us the unpretentious attitudes of the two women mentioned in the New Testament who washed and anointed Jesus' feet. They were willing to humble themselves in His presence. Both women trusted this man from Galilee—one had faith in His authority to forgive, the other believed in His power over death.

Thank You, Lord, for giving me that hope of Your forgiveness and the belief in eternal life.

I pray, dear Lord, that You will let me be a small footstool for Christ, to live beneath the shadow of His splendid radiance. Oh, that I could weep enough tears from my own repentance to bathe His feet and anoint them with the sweet perfume of my joyful heart!

I pray all things in His name. Amen.

Fragrance

*But thanks be to God, who. . .uses us to spread
the aroma of the knowledge of him everywhere.
For we are to God the pleasing aroma of Christ.*

2 CORINTHIANS 2:14–15 NIV

Dear God, sometimes I stink! I was snarly with the cashier. I
yelled at my kids. Again. You were not evident to others through
me. I'm sorry for my sins of the tongue, bad attitudes, and neglect
of You. Wean me from myself: self-reliance, self-promotion,
self-indulgence. With age, I thought I would sin less because of
greater maturity and strength; instead, I have more awareness of
my need for wisdom and understanding to guard my heart and
control my thoughts. Forgive my willful sins and hidden faults.
Thank You that my sins were blotted out at the cross, and You
keep no record of them. You are faithful and just to forgive me
and purify me from all unrighteousness.

May I offer You the precious ointment of devotional living,
poured on Your feet so the fragrance fills up whatever room I am
in. May I overflow Your love and kindness to my family, friends,
and even strangers. May unbelievers be drawn to You when they
"smell" me. Please use me to help complete the body of Christ.
Because You fill all in all, fill me with Yourself so I can overflow
to others who need You in this age, so they will be with You in
the age to come. Amen.

Hope Still

One of the sons of [Elam] spoke up and said to Ezra,
"We have trespassed against our God, and have taken
pagan wives from the peoples of the land; yet now
there is hope in Israel in spite of this."

EZRA 10:2 NKJV

Eternal hope, I come to You now in the abundance of Your steadfast love; answer me. What strength do I have that I should hope? Brokenness seems to ensnare everyone and everything around me. I, too, fall prey to the sins that so easily ensnare all creatures. I am an unfaithful bride to my Groom, who is Christ. Like Your people Israel long ago, I also let the ways of nonbelievers corrupt my heart. Instead of distancing themselves from sin, the Israelites accepted it among them; and I do the same. However, I praise You, Abba, for forgiving and for turning the hearts of Your children back to You. Even in the darkest of places You give hope by calling people to You through faith in Jesus. In spite of all the evil and rebellion against God in the world, Jesus continues the work of redemption. Thank You for this hope that You have delivered to me and continue to deliver to Your Church. Let this hope make me bold and put an end to the sin in my actions. I have no strength to do this on my own; but I hope in the strength of Christ through His victory over sin and death.

Your Faithfulness

*Trust in the LORD and do good; dwell in
the land, and feed on His faithfulness.*
PSALM 37:3 NKJV

God, it encourages me to know that I don't need to rely on my own faithfulness, but can absolutely rely on Yours! I know I fail, and will fail again, no matter how hard I try to get it right. When I trust in You and count on the character of who You are—faithful—instead of my own weak flesh, then I can rest in the certainty that Your Spirit will work and move in my life.

When I "feed" on Your faithfulness and not on my own abilities—or lack thereof—but on the promises You have kept already, my faith is strengthened. The Israelites were encouraged to "dwell in the land"—the land that You had not only promised, but delivered to them. Lord, You were faithful then; You are faithful now.

When I count all the times You have kept Your word, Lord, I am feeding on Your faithfulness and reminding myself that whatever I am facing at this moment You will continue to follow through and do what You have said. That's just who You are—and You never change!

Thank You, Lord, for these words from the Psalms that encourage me to continue on, to trust in You. I need this reminder daily as I endeavor to be faithful to You. Amen.

Wisdom Only from God

So we have not stopped praying for you since we first heard about you. We ask God to give you complete knowledge of his will and to give you spiritual wisdom and understanding.

COLOSSIANS 1:9 NLT

Lord, thank You for making wisdom and understanding available to me. Do not let me believe the lie and think that I am wise of my own ability. Instead, teach me to trust You and lean on Your wisdom. One way that I know I can walk in Your wisdom is to acknowledge You in everything I do and say.

I lean completely on You. I rest on and trust that You know what is best for me. You want only good for me, and I refuse to be wise in my own eyes. I want to always stay ready and open to hear from You.

Thank You for those You have put in my life who love me and want Your best for me. I know that there are times when I want to go my own way, and You have put it in their hearts to pray for me that I might choose Your wisdom instead of my own selfish plans.

I trust You and am ready to be corrected by Your Word. I bring my decisions to You in prayer and choose the Bible as my guide. I know You will make Your direction and counsel known to me as I seek to do things Your way.

Absolutely True

For we were not making up clever stories when we told you about the powerful coming of our Lord Jesus Christ. We saw his majestic splendor with our own eyes when he received honor and glory from God the Father. The voice from the majestic glory of God said to him, "This is my dearly loved Son, who brings me great joy." We ourselves heard that voice from heaven when we were with him on the holy mountain. Because of that experience, we have even greater confidence in the message proclaimed by the prophets. You must pay close attention to what they wrote, for their words are like a lamp shining in a dark place—until the Day dawns, and Christ the Morning Star shines in your hearts. Above all, you must realize that no prophecy in Scripture ever came from the prophet's own understanding, or from human initiative. No, those prophets were moved by the Holy Spirit, and they spoke from God.

2 PETER 1:16–21 NLT

Oh Lord, this passage is such an encouragement to me. Bring me back to it anytime critics of Your Word start to wear me down and make me wonder if maybe the Bible really is just a book of made-up stories. Strengthen my faith that every word of the Bible is inspired by You and it is useful and powerful for guiding my life to You. You've shown me this in the past, but I need to hear it again and again. Please don't stop reminding me. Help me cling to the power of Your Word, confident that it is absolutely true, absolutely from You.

Faithful One

Jesus Christ is the same yesterday, today, and forever.
Hebrews 13:8 NLT

Dear heavenly Father, throughout my life You've blessed me with an abundance of friends. You designed me to enjoy relationships through time spent with people. I crave face-to-face conversations. They don't happen too often because of busy lives, others' and mine. A few moments at church, on the phone, or by email doesn't quite satisfy me. But brief contact is better than no contact.

I feel the loss of friends deeply. Those who move build new lives, and I'm less and less a part of them. Others stay, but change in life situations limit time for visits. And how I miss two prayer partners who are with You now. We grew in You through good times and bad.

A coworker's betrayal shocked me. We'd been friends for years. At least I thought we were. I felt like I'd been kicked in the gut. Has she received Jesus yet?

My husband's my best friend. I know one of us may be left alone through death. That earthly loss will be the deepest grief. But, praise God, we'll spend eternity together.

People change. Circumstances change. Life is full of lows and highs. I lose friends and make new ones. The only constant in my life is You, Lord. You never change. You'll never leave me. You'll always love me. And, You're preparing a place for me in heaven. Thank You for sweet assurance of seeing Christian friends and family again.

Loving Those Who Are Difficult to Love

*"If you love those who love you, what reward will you get?
Are not even the tax collectors doing that? And if you greet
only your own people, what are you doing more than others?
Do not even pagans do that? Be perfect, therefore,
as your heavenly Father is perfect."*

MATTHEW 5:46–48 NIV

Heavenly Father, why is it so hard for me to love everyone?
That's what You want me to do, but every day I encounter
difficult people who are difficult to love. Some are rude, Lord,
shoving their way past me, hurrying to get where they want to
go. Others are selfish, wanting what they want without thinking
of what I need. A few are uncaring and unappreciative of the
things that I do for them. I want to love them, God, but it's hard
when they hurt me or put me into a bad mood. But wait—You
whisper to me, "Have you ever been rude, selfish, uncaring, or
unappreciative?" Yes Lord, I have. Thank You for reminding
me. There are times when I am in a hurry and not thinking of
those around me. I have wanted selfishly and have forgotten to
show appreciation for the little things that others do. Forgive
me, Lord. I can be difficult to love, too! Help me to love others
perfectly, as You love them, with patience, kindness, forgiveness,
and understanding. And help me, please, to be easier to love.
In Jesus' name, I pray. Amen.

Surrounded by God's Unfailing Love

Therefore let all the faithful pray to you while you may be found; surely the rising of the mighty waters will not reach them. You are my hiding place; you will protect me from trouble and surround me with songs of deliverance. I will instruct you and teach you in the way you should go; I will counsel you with my loving eye on you. . . . Many are the woes of the wicked, but the LORD's unfailing love surrounds the one who trusts in him.

PSALM 32:6–8, 10 NIV

Lord, there is no one like You to help the powerless against the mighty. Help us, Lord our God, for we rely on You. Give me strength and courage to be Your faithful servant as I seek You with all my heart. When I feel like hiding, Lord, remind me that I can find solace and comfort in You. Please protect me from trouble, and give me theme songs of praise to cling to as I wait upon You.

I am so grateful that You, the Creator of all, will give me wisdom and that You will counsel me Yourself. Sometimes it's so hard to believe that You actually have Your loving eye on *me*! But Your Word says it is true, and I choose to believe it. I know that Your unfailing love surrounds me at all times. I praise You and love You for that promise!

Forgiven

*Watch out that no poisonous root of bitterness
grows up to trouble you, corrupting many.*
HEBREWS 12:15 NLT

Generous God, You even gave Your only begotten Son to die so I can live eternally with You. Help me to be generous and self-sacrificing, too. Enable me to give and to give up. To deny my flesh so I can walk in the Spirit. To forgive because I am forgiven. I confess that I desire to hold a grudge against the person who caused me so much pain. Will I ever stop grieving the loss? Hiding the shame? Or wanting that person to change? Please change me. Cleanse me from my stubborn desire for revenge. I know my offender and I can never be friends, but I want to stop being enemies. Prevent me from focusing on past hurts.

In obedience to You, I ask You to forgive my enemy for all offenses against me. I need the working of Your mighty power to put this to death and to resurrect my emotions and motives with freedom to move on and be controlled by this no longer. Help my enemy also to seek Your forgiveness and emotional healing, even if we never speak again. Because I have experienced a minute and brief portion of what Christ suffered, You have promised that I will also share His glory. I rejoice in Your undeserved favor. Thank You for understanding everything I feel. I am weak; You are my daily Strength. Amen.

By His Authority

God has put all things under the authority of Christ and has
made him head over all things for the benefit of the church.
EPHESIANS 1:22 NLT

Gracious Father in heaven, Jesus Christ gave sight to blind
men to provide irrefutable evidence of His authority on earth
to forgive. By His authority, He commanded lame men to walk.
And, by His authority, they got up and walked, liberated from
their debilitating ailments by Christ's forgiving love.

I was once blind to Christ's love and spiritually crippled
before I accepted His forgiveness. Feeling my way in the darkness, I didn't even realize how blind I was until He touched my
soul and opened my eyes. The first images I saw were my sins
and the ugliness of my life. But Jesus' forgiveness covered over
those repulsive visions like a blanket covering a smoldering fire.
And, by His authority, they are buried forever. I now walk in the
brightness of life knowing He is always with me.

I give thanks to You, Father, for Christ's authority to forgive
me, which has given me the authority to come to You in prayer.

Help me to show my spiritually blind and crippled friends
and loved ones what a precious gift we receive when we yield
to the Savior's authority. Let me show them the eternal hope
for a future in heaven.

I pray in the name and authority of Jesus. Amen.

Confident Hope

---

*My dear friends, we are already God's children, though what we
will be hasn't yet been seen. But we do know that when Christ
returns, we will be like him, because we will see him as he truly
is. This hope makes us keep ourselves holy, just as Christ is holy.*

1 JOHN 3:2–3 CEV

"This hope" that I have in You, Lord, is enough to carry me
through anything. Knowing I am already Your child and that
one day I will be like Jesus is a hope, a certainty. We wait, as
Paul says in Romans 8:23 (NLT), "with eager hope for the day
when God will give us our full rights as his adopted children."
The powerful truth of knowing we were saved in this hope makes
us wait with patience and confidence (hope).

Father, I confess that I am not always as confident in this
hope as I should be. My eyes too often are focused on the here
and now, not the future, not eternity. Help me remember that
eternity has already begun for me. This life here on earth is
temporary, and even if I live what is considered to be a long life,
it won't even be a blip on eternity's radar screen.

As 2 Corinthians 4:17–18 tells me, the glory that awaits
far exceeds whatever difficulties I may face now. Lord, I ask for
patience and insight, a fresh perspective on what this life looks
like from the other side. Amen.

Doing the Word

Do not merely listen to the word, and so deceive yourselves.
Do what it says. Anyone who listens to the word but does not do
what it says is like someone who looks at his face in a mirror and,
after looking at himself, goes away and immediately forgets what
he looks like. But whoever looks intently into the perfect law that
gives freedom, and continues in it—not forgetting what they have
heard, but doing it—they will be blessed in what they do.

JAMES 1:22–25 NIV

God, I don't want to be a foolish person who can look in the mirror but when I walk away immediately forget what I look like. Nor do I want to be able to walk away from Your Word and forget it. I want to study it and follow it and live it out in my life. It's no easy task, but I truly want to "*do what it says.*"

When I am reading the Bible, listening to a sermon, or participating in a Bible study, please keep me attentive to how You want me to apply it to my life. Soften my heart to receive Your instruction. Perk my ears to be listening for Your voice. Open my eyes to be watching for Your hand at work in all situations. Teach me Your Word in every way possible! Let it change me and mature me and spur me to action.

Authority of Christ

And He put all things under His feet, and gave
Him to be head over all things to the church.

EPHESIANS 1:22 NKJV

King of kings, You who are without beginning, Alpha and Omega, humbled Yourself so You might show the foolishness of human strivings and pride. You, born in little Bethlehem and raised in scorned Nazareth, are the promised Branch of Jesse. Your power is the only true power, and it is found in meekness, humility, and death. Test my heart and mold it to match that of my beautiful King. You reign in the hearts of men and women who diligently seek You; and it is a reign without end. How can the Creator be limited? Jesus, You are one with God, and stop me from ever acting as though Your power is anything less than perfect, holy, complete, and eternal. Keep me from forgetting that You reign over the powers and principalities, over all might and dominion. I hold on to Your name as Your child. It is the name that is above every name, at which every knee will bow. Let many come to know and worship You now before it is too late; and let me join them in glorifying God by confessing that Jesus is Lord. Renew in me awe and obedience. Jesus has crushed the serpent's head by innocently dying and then overcoming death. Guide me to live in the truth that You, Father, put all things under Christ's authority.

More Than Words

We always thank God, the Father of our Lord Jesus Christ,
when we pray for you, because we have heard of your faith
in Christ Jesus and of the love you have for all God's people.
COLOSSIANS 1:3–4 NIV

God, thank You for the opportunity to know You intimately. I want to know You more and more each day. I feel guilty when I let the day slip away and I haven't spent time in Your presence. There are so many ways I can know You more. When I read about You and about Jesus Christ in the Bible, please make Your Word come alive in me. Let me read it, comprehend it, and understand what You want to tell me about Yourself through the written Word.

When I pray, let my words be more than a quick blessing for the food or a prayer for the day. Help me to speak from my heart, but even more importantly, remind me to pause and listen to what You have to say to me from deep within.

As I go about my day, I want to stay aware that You are with me at all times. I can tap into Your wisdom for each decision I need to make. I can breathe a prayer for the things that come up and concern me. I open my heart and give You all of me. I surrender to You all the places of my heart and choose to grow closer to You in everything I say and do today.

Temptation

*"Watch and pray so that you will not fall into temptation.
The spirit is willing, but the flesh is weak."*
MATTHEW 26:41 NIV

Merciful Father, I've failed again. I've failed myself, but mostly I've failed You. I don't know how You are so patient with me. Help me to recognize my weakness, resist temptation, and rely on You for power. You are the only One I can talk to about this. Sometimes I wonder if this is my thorn in the flesh. Such an irritation. Makes me long for my resurrection body. But all in Your time. I need to realize You are sufficient for me today.

Trying to resist temptation on my own doesn't work. Help me remember the consequences. Instant pleasure eventually turns into regret and guilt and brings forth death—the death of my fellowship with You. Most holy God, search my heart, and help me deal ruthlessly with sin. Make me realize how much it grieves You. I'm ashamed of myself and I'm sorry. You have promised my temptations will not be more than I can bear because You provide a way of escape—help me to escape by saying no. By resisting peer pressure. By denying my carnal desires. Retrain my brain to focus on truth. Show me the exceeding greatness of Your power.

How I need to rely on that. I can only be strong when I am weak and helplessly dependent on You. Thank You for mercy and forgiveness. Amen.

Faithful Father

Let us hold fast the confession of our hope without wavering, for He who promised is faithful.
HEBREWS 10:23 NKJV

Dear Father, I just heard on the radio about the American pastor who's still in prison for his faith. He's in a country far away. At odd moments he comes to mind, and I pray for him. You don't remind me of people and situations to merely think about or feel sorry for. Many times I pray that he knows Your love at that minute. It must be almost unbearable to be held captive in such horrible conditions. Father, please hold him when his hope wavers.

I pray for the pastor's wife as she raises their children alone. Fear and despair probably attempt to smother her at times. They won't win! Please encourage her heart. You know her better than she knows herself. Please touch her in a personal way. Flood her with confidence in the hope You've given her.

Bless this dear couple today. I don't know what that would look like, but You do. Thank You for the privilege of praying for them. They love You and are called by You. I'm sure You can somehow turn this for good (Romans 8:28 NIV).

Believers in the persecuted Church are part of the body. How many are suffering today? The enemy tries to intimidate me into feeling helpless. Yet, I am *not* helpless. I can pray to our listening heavenly Father for His precious children.

God's Power at Work through Me

Now all glory to God, who is able, through his mighty power at work within us, to accomplish infinitely more than we might ask or think.

EPHESIANS 3:20 NLT

Dear God, the apostle Paul teaches that Your mighty power works within us to accomplish infinitely more than we might ask or think. Infinitely! The possibilities are endless. God, how can I help You? I can think of ways to help in my church, my community, and even the world, but Your ideas are infinitely more creative than mine. Use Your power to think for me. If my ideas are too small, then show me how to make them grow. If they are too grand, then teach me to simplify them. Remind me that sometimes the simplest acts are the most helpful—kind words, listening, understanding, befriending someone who is lonely or sick. Use Your power within me to excel at these things. Encourage me to work diligently for You. When You give me a task and something blocks my way, remove it. Allow Your power to flow through me when I am weary. Give me strength to press on toward Your goal. If You ask me to step out in faith into some new territory, then use Your power to calm me and help me to move beyond my comfort zone. God, whatever it is that You ask me to do, I will do it selflessly and to You I will give all the glory. In Jesus' name, I pray. Amen.

The Joy of Knowing God

*Rejoice in the Lord always. I will say it again: Rejoice!
Let your gentleness be evident to all. The Lord is near.*

PHILIPPIANS 4:4–5 NIV

Heavenly Father, I rejoice because You are near. I know You see me and hear my prayers. I can't describe the joy and hope I have knowing that You care about every little thing in my life. . . and that You want to hear all about it! I want to find out what pleases You, Lord. And I ask that You help me have the courage to obey You in every circumstance.

As Your Word tells me, You have brought me out of darkness and now I am light—in You! And that's a reason to rejoice *always*! Help me to live as a child of the light and to serve You in goodness, righteousness, and truth. Let others see that I am gentle and not forceful as I share the joy of my salvation with them. Put a check in my spirit when I feel the need to argue my own opinion in ways that aren't pleasing to You. I know You want me to stand and live for what is right, but please help me do that in a gentle and respectful way.

Thank You for the great joy I have in knowing and serving You.

Handing Over Control

The Son is the image of the invisible God, the firstborn over all creation. For in him all things were created: things in heaven and on earth, visible and invisible, whether thrones or powers or rulers or authorities; all things have been created through him and for him. He is before all things, and in him all things hold together.

COLOSSIANS 1:15–17 NIV

Father God, according to Ephesians 1:22 You have put all things under Christ. He rules and reigns over everything. Why, then, is it so hard at times to recognize His authority and power? I know the world doesn't recognize Jesus for who He is—Your Son—but God, I know who He is and I can still fail to acknowledge His authority!

My mind can scarcely comprehend what this means. I'm not in control, never will be, but I don't need to be in control. I only need to trust and believe in the One who is. I think Paul's prayer in Ephesians is for that recognition. Because if I truly believe that Christ is in all and over all, then I will rest in Him alone, knowing I don't need to worry: He can handle it. If only I could live in this truth every moment of my life!

God, may every step of my faith journey bring me closer to You. Help me when I stumble, fear, doubt, or neglect the discipline of loving and serving You. Amen.

Building the Body

*And appointed him to be head over everything for
the church, which is his body, the fullness of
him who fills everything in every way.*
EPHESIANS 1:22–23 NIV

Gracious Lord, Jesus made peace with us through His shed blood at the cross. Because of our belief in Christ, we are now the Church. It isn't a building made with bricks, stones, or wood, but the body of the risen Christ. Each believer in the congregation is an individual member of that body. You have assigned some of us to be arms to embrace one another in Christian love. Others are legs to take steps to move us forward in our Bible study. Some are eyes to see the vision of Your design. Some members serve as ears to listen and discern the teaching we receive. And some are lips to speak the word of truth.

Thank You for showing us how to make our churches miniatures of the body of Christ. We serve You, Lord, as pastors, elders, teachers, evangelists, and even musicians. We want to use the talents that You have given us to equip others to grow in their faith and serve You, too.

Let us be filled with the fullness of Him in all we do as we strive for the level of maturity in our belief and acceptance of the Son to become unified as one body, reaching toward the wholehearted fullness of Christ.

In His precious name, I pray. Amen.

Healing

> *"The LORD gave, and the LORD has taken away;*
> *may the name of the LORD be praised."*
>
> JOB 1:21 NIV

God of my losses, I know I can't have heaven on earth, but You are my safe place here. My perfect Father who never makes a mistake, never has second thoughts. You do everything right the first time. Your ways are right, but incomprehensible. I do accept Your will, even if healing never comes in this life. However, because of the exceeding greatness of Your power, the power that raised Christ from the dead and exalted Him over all, I humbly ask for complete healing and recovery. Your will be done, not mine.

God of all comfort, I may never know Your good purposes until eternity. Help me to remember that my afflictions are not permanent. I won't have them forever—only for earth. You will give grace to help every time I need it. But if I can serve You better and testify of Your goodness by being healed, then please restore me in Your time. You are my loving God—Your nature is love. Every mark You make on my life and body and on those dear to me is a love mark. As Christ is head over His body, the Church, so may I keep Him as head over me and my body—all my physical and emotional needs, my mind and will, attitudes and choices. Till Jesus comes or I myself see Him in glory. Amen.

Faithful Fellowship

I thank my God upon every remembrance of you, always in every prayer of mine making request for you all with joy, for your fellowship in the gospel from the first day until now, being confident of this very thing, that He who has begun a good work in you will complete it until the day of Jesus Christ; just as it is right for me to think this of you all, because I have you in my heart, inasmuch as both in my chains and in the defense and confirmation of the gospel, you all are partakers with me of grace.

PHILIPPIANS 1:3–7 NKJV

Lord, I am so thankful for other believers, for brothers and sisters in Christ and the encouragement, love, and support they give me. The community of faith is one that continues to bring joy and comfort. Beyond surface relationships, the bond of Christ unites heart with heart in a way that only the Holy Spirit can do.

When we pray for one another we invest in others' lives. We partake of the same grace, and this strengthens not just relationships but our own faith as well. We share in others' joys and sorrows, and this brings deep friendship that can only be explained supernaturally.

Thank You for letting me experience this, Lord. Help me to pray for others in the faith to experience it as well, that believers would live in community with one another and with You. Amen.

Spirit of Wisdom

That the God of our Lord Jesus Christ, the Father
of glory, may give to you the spirit of wisdom
and revelation in the knowledge of Him.
EPHESIANS 1:17 NKJV

Heavenly Father, from the earliest of times Your presence and wisdom were evident in those who obeyed You. Your Spirit guided Joseph to interpret Pharaoh's dreams. Guide the state leaders of today with that Spirit. You filled Moses and Joshua with the spirit of wisdom to lead Your children out of slavery. Fill the shepherds of today's Church with wisdom to bring people out of sin's slavery. This same spirit of wisdom propelled Daniel to declare clearly God's plan and speak boldly against the king of Babylon. Raise such steadfast and courageous leaders today as You did in the past. Let the spirit given to Elijah turn the hearts of fathers to their children, and let Your wisdom bring reconciliation and greater unity in my own family. Your Spirit and wisdom so beautifully convicted and built up the apostles. May the pastors of today live lives worthy of Your calling. Thank You for providing a host of examples of people to whom You gave Your wisdom: Ruth, Samuel, David, Solomon, Isaiah. I mourn for those who, though they know Your wisdom, choose to rebel against it. I praise You that the Spirit never gives up. Thank You for the perfect example of obedience to Your spirit of wisdom—Jesus. Pour this wisdom into my own heart and mind.

God at Work in Me

In Him you also trusted, after you heard the word of truth,
the gospel of your salvation; in whom also, having believed,
you were sealed with the Holy Spirit of promise.

EPHESIANS 1:13 NKJV

Heavenly Father, thank You for the gift of the Holy Spirit at work in me. His power and peace confirms that I belong to You. It is proof of the promise of my salvation and redemption. His presence in me demonstrates the genuineness of my faith and proves that I am a child of God. His power is always at work in me, and I ask that His power flows through me so that I can be a light in the lives of others around me.

I pray my choices and decisions compel others to come to know You. I cannot do that alone, but through my faith and trust in You that the Holy Spirit will be my helper, You give me the strength and wisdom I need to do all that You have set before me.

I ask You, Father, to continue to transform my life today. Show me how to make the changes I need to in order to be more like You. Help me to see Your purpose and plan and know Your desires for my life as the Holy Spirit leads, guides, and teaches me today. I trust You to do the things necessary to help me become all that You've destined me to be.

The Good Life

*Dear friends, you are foreigners and strangers on this earth. So
I beg you not to surrender to those desires that fight against you.
Always let others see you behaving properly, even though they
may still accuse you of doing wrong. Then on the day of judgment,
they will honor God by telling the good things they saw you do.*

1 PETER 2:11–12 CEV

Father, please help me to make my life a testimony that points
others to You and brings You glory. Let me strive for holiness
in all that I do. I need Your strength and wisdom in order to
flee from sin. Arm me with Your strength and Your Word so
that I'm ready to do battle with the evil that will tempt me. It's
so easy to give in to the lusts of this world, but I want to live
among nonbelievers in such a good and loving way that they
can't help but see You in me and want to know more about
You. I want to inspire others, to show them that yielding to sin
results in bad consequences but avoiding sin results in many
kinds of blessings from You.

Help me to be a light in a dark place without being consumed
by the darkness. I can't do this alone, Father. I need You, and I
need You to encourage me with like-minded believers who help
keep me accountable.

A Love-Filled Life

*Imitate God, therefore, in everything you do, because you
are his dear children. Live a life filled with love, following
the example of Christ. He loved us and offered himself
as a sacrifice for us, a pleasing aroma to God.*

EPHESIANS 5:1–2 NLT

Dear God, *grrrrr*. The man is maddening. Once again he almost
ran me over in the coffee shop. No eye contact. No "Excuse
me." He charged past me toward the counter to order his usual.
Whatever that is. I certainly don't know and don't care. But I
see the baristas do. It's already made for him.

For years that man has ignored me. The only time he ever
spoke was when I stepped into his path and said, "Good morning."
After I got a mumbled greeting, if you can call it that, I moved
out of his way. He's just rude. What's wrong with him?

Hmmm. What's wrong with me? How can I allow his actions
to plunge me into a snit? You've been silent through my tirade.
Let me try this again. Lord, what *is* wrong with him? Have I
offended him? Is he shy, or is he merely in a hurry?

It's still mighty quiet. Well, not entirely quiet. I keep hearing the word *love*. I know You love him. But me love him? He's
such a jerk. Oops. There I go again. I want to please You, Father.
But it's impossible. I can't imitate You without Your help. Holy
Spirit, help!

Joyful Thanksgiving

We continually ask God to fill you with the knowledge of his will through all the wisdom and understanding that the Spirit gives, so that you may live a life worthy of the Lord and please him in every way: bearing fruit in every good work, growing in the knowledge of God, being strengthened with all power according to his glorious might so that you may have great endurance and patience, and giving joyful thanks to the Father, who has qualified you to share in the inheritance of his holy people in the kingdom of light.

COLOSSIANS 1:9–12 NIV

Oh Lord, I am filled with joyful praise! Thank You for the inheritance You have promised to me, Your child. I am grateful that You chose me! How privileged I am to be adopted into Your family. You sent Your Son, Jesus, to save me so that I can be holy and blameless in Your sight! You forgive me for my sins, and You love me unconditionally all the time. Every day, You pour infinite blessings upon me; I have all that I need. Thank You, Father, for these mighty gifts. You have opened my eyes to the perfect truth that You rule heaven and earth, and best of all that You have made a home for me in heaven. Oh God! I praise You for Your faithfulness. I thank You for loving me and making me a part of Your family. Amen.

Walking in Love and Strength

But the Lord is faithful; he will strengthen you and guard
you from the evil one. And we are confident in the Lord
that you are doing and will continue to do the things we
commanded you. May the Lord lead your hearts into a
full understanding and expression of the love of God
and the patient endurance that comes from Christ.

2 THESSALONIANS 3:3–5 NLT

Lord, I know that our enemy wants to defeat me. His plan is to steal, kill, and destroy. I pray that You will strengthen me with the same power that raised Christ from the dead. I feel inadequate and weak sometimes. I trip up over the same things again and again. I am ashamed of my lack of self-control in certain areas. I ask Your forgiveness for when I fail. Show me a new way, and allow me to lean on You when I am at my weakest.

Please lead my heart into a full understanding of Your love. I want to know You more and allow You to take control of every thought and action that I pursue. Show me the strongholds in my life that I need to surrender to You. I don't want to give the enemy a foothold in my life. Purify my heart and cleanse me from the sins that are clouding my relationship with You. Help me to walk in Your love and strength.

The Key

*But may all who search for you be filled with joy
and gladness in you. May those who love your
salvation repeatedly shout, "God is great!"*
PSALM 70:4 NLT

Father, You promise that if I seek You with my whole heart You
will be found (Jeremiah 29:13). The key is that I must be looking
for You in the ordinariness of my every day. Too often I fail to
thank You. There are so many things in my life that I take for
granted and don't recognize Your providence and care for me.
The psalmist tells me that when my concentration is where it
should be, then I can acknowledge You, and this always brings
joy and thankfulness.

God, You are indeed great—whether I feel like admitting
that or not! When I think of Your salvation and all that You offer
me through it—love, mercy, grace, Your righteousness—then
everything else falls into its proper place and perspective.

Today, Lord, may I just thank You for loving me enough
to save me? May I be reminded of all that You have given me.
It is more than "enough." It far exceeds what my mind can
comprehend! "No eye has seen, no ear has heard, and no mind
has imagined what God has prepared for those who love him"
(1 Corinthians 2:9 NLT).

You give me every reason to rejoice and to praise You, Lord.
May I be faithful in loving and serving You. Amen.

In the Fullness of His Plenty

Which is his body, the fullness of him
who fills everything in every way.
EPHESIANS 1:23 NIV

Our gracious and loving God, too many times we look for fulfillment in our earthly existence. We put our hope and trust into our careers, hobbies, or leisure activities, only to be greatly disappointed when they fall short of our desires. These temporal bits and pieces can never satisfy our need for Your presence in our lives.

Jesus Christ took Your fullness in bodily form to make peace with Your rebellious creation. He reconciled us to You through His death, resurrection, and ascension. There is no more fulfilling love than that.

I pray for the fullness of Your love to open our hearts, Lord, that we may realize Christ's fullness in all our experiences in Christian living. Our lives should be overflowing with the hope, joy, and peace You want to share with us. Let us learn to value Christ's love, which is the only fulfilling experience we can appreciate in life.

Thank You, Father, for Jesus Christ, our Savior who fills us with grace upon grace, even though we don't deserve it. Please help us to firmly hold on to that abundant blessing. Only then will we be truly satisfied.

I pray this in the name of our precious Lord, Jesus. Amen.

Pleasing Faith

Faith makes us sure of what we hope for and gives us proof
of what we cannot see. It was their faith that made our
ancestors pleasing to God. . . . Because Noah had faith,
he was warned about something that had not yet happened.
He obeyed and built a boat that saved him and his family.

HEBREWS 11:1–2, 7 CEV

It is faith that pleases You, God (Hebrews 11:6), and without it
we cannot even be Your children. Noah trusted You. He believed
in what You said to him and was obedient even though he was
probably thought of as a fool by his contemporaries. Obedience
builds faith and gives strength for the spiritual battle. Faith is
not easy; it moves beyond what we can see with our eyes. It is
belief and trust in spite of circumstance or what others might
say or believe.

Paul talks about walking "by faith" (2 Corinthians 5:7 NIV)
and not by sight—but my faith in You is not "blind"! You have
kept promise after promise and have transformed my life—I
know You are trustworthy. But I admit that sometimes I stumble. Sometimes having insight into the spiritual realm over the
physical one can be difficult. But every step of faith I take, You
grant me strength to trust You more.

Walk with me, Lord, on this journey toward You. As I live
in the present, help me see the bigger picture—with eyes on
eternity instead of this world. Amen.

Others First

*Is there any encouragement from belonging to Christ? Any
comfort from his love? Any fellowship together in the Spirit?
Are your hearts tender and compassionate? Then make me truly
happy by agreeing wholeheartedly with each other, loving one
another, and working together with one mind and purpose.
Don't be selfish; don't try to impress others. Be humble, thinking
of others as better than yourselves. Don't look out only for your
own interests, but take an interest in others, too.*

PHILIPPIANS 2:1–4 NLT

Lord, thinking of myself first is the easy thing to do. It's what
always feels right to my sinful nature, to look out for number
one. But Your Word tells me to consider others before myself
and take an interest in them. It's so much easier said than done!

Please help me to get my eyes off myself and instead focus
on the needs of those around me. There are so many, Lord—so
many that sometimes it just feels pointless because the needs
are so great, and I wonder what I can possibly do to make a difference. Please help me fight that discouragement. Help me not
to grow weary in doing good. Give me strength and endurance
to keep on serving others, just like You did in Your time here on
earth. Remind me that whatever I do for others, I am ultimately
doing for You. Help me not to lose heart but to find great joy in
blessing others. Give me confidence that as I am helping meet the
needs of others, You will be providing for all my needs as well.

A God Moment

*Kind words are like honey—sweet to
the soul and healthy for the body.*
PROVERBS 16:24 NLT

Dear heavenly Father, thank You for a pleasant surprise this morning. A young man just told me to have a great day. A teenager.

The whole experience with that couple was lovely. It's unusual to see a high school student at five thirty in the morning. When he came into the coffee shop, I felt territorial defenses rising when he headed for my table. Of course, it's the community table, and he sat at the opposite end. Nevertheless, it's my table. Any of the regulars would say so.

I smiled at him, but he was buried in his work. I shrugged and returned to my Bible reading. Then the girl arrived. I braced for loud conversation. However, the two talked softly, so I continued my quiet time.

When they began packing up, I asked if they were doing homework. We chatted for a minute or two. They're high school seniors. I asked if they had senioritis yet. She said that he does. I told him to hold on. It won't be long.

Both kids smiled at me before they left. As he walked past me, he wished me a good day. Our brief interaction warmed my heart.

Lord, I don't know them, but You do. I pray that each one will walk in the plan You've designed for their lives. And that they will come to know Your unconditional, deep love.

Faithful with the Gift of Salvation

In whom we have redemption through his blood,
the forgiveness of sins, according to the riches of his grace.

EPHESIANS 1:7 KJV

Heavenly Father, thank You for Your grace. I know there is nothing I could have done to earn salvation, but it's by Your grace that Jesus willingly made the exchange. He took all my sin and counted me without sin. Through the forgiveness of my sin by His redemptive blood, I am free to live my life each day in Your presence.

Help me to remember that salvation is not just a ticket to heaven, but so much more. I must make a daily decision to accept the gift of salvation. I am free to live my life free from the cares of this world because Jesus took all the cares upon Himself. I am free from my past because You washed my past away. Each day You look at me as the new creature I am in Christ.

I want to grow and become the new person You have created me to be. Today I choose to accept Your grace. Continue to teach me to live my life in a way that honors You and brings glory to You. I will honor the sacrifice that Jesus made for my salvation by doing those things that bring You pleasure. Thank You again, Father, for Your great gift of grace.

A Life of Purpose

All praise to God, the Father of our Lord Jesus Christ. It is by his great mercy that we have been born again, because God raised Jesus Christ from the dead. Now we live with great expectation, and we have a priceless inheritance— an inheritance that is kept in heaven for you, pure and undefiled, beyond the reach of change and decay.

1 PETER 1:3–4 NLT

Lord, when I think of the inheritance I receive in Christ—one that cannot be corrupted by anything—I fall on my knees and thank You! Knowing what my future holds brings me confidence to live today and brings peace and stability to a shifting, changing world. I have no control in many areas of my life—but eternity is sure and certain and puts everything into perspective for me. What I do now is important, but everything here on earth is temporary.

Jesus tells us in Matthew not to store up treasure on earth because it can be destroyed or stolen (Matthew 6:19). The real treasure is the one that lives on in eternity. It is easy to get caught up in the day-to-day act of survival, but am I so involved in the material side of life that I am neglecting what really matters?

Father, I need Your help to see the world through the lens of Your Word. I want Your perspective on life here so that I might do all I can to live out a life of purpose. Amen.

God's Peace

Don't worry about anything; instead, pray about everything.
Tell God what you need, and thank him for all he has done.
Then you will experience God's peace, which exceeds anything
we can understand. His peace will guard your hearts
and minds as you live in Christ Jesus.

PHILIPPIANS 4:6–7 NLT

Thank You, heavenly Father, that I have nothing to fear or worry about when You are on my side. Instead of being afraid and getting anxious, You ask that I pray and tell You what I need. You make it clear to me what I'm supposed to be doing during difficult times. My heart is heavy over several things, and I lay them down at the foot of the cross. I have some burdens that feel like they are too much for me. There are situations and people in my life that I don't know how to deal with in a way that honors You.

Please give me wisdom and peace as I bring my needs before You. Please help me remember that I've experienced a lifetime of Your love and faithfulness. Help me remember that You won't ever leave me or forsake me. I thank You and praise You for all You have done in my life. You have brought me out of darkness and into Your marvelous light. Please bless me with the peace that only You can offer. Guard my heart and my mind as I put my trust in You, Lord.

Scripture Index

If You Liked This Book, Check Out...

1,001 Prayers to Energize Your Prayer Life

Prayer is a powerful privilege given to Christians, but we often struggle to know where to start. Here, readers will find hundreds of uplifting and challenging prayer starters in *1,001 Prayers to Energize Your Prayer Life*. This compact book offers simple, heartfelt prayers for many of life's situations, and readers will find just the right pick-me-up for daily conversations with their heavenly Father.

Paperback / 978-1-68322-345-0 / $5.99

Prayers with Purpose for Women

This practical and powerful prayer guide helps women begin or end their days by offering specific prayer starters for 21 key areas of life. Topical chapters include emotions, home, health, work, finances, career, and family and are complemented by relevant scripture selections.

Paperback / 978-1-61626-869-5 / $4.99